Espionage
and Intelligence

D0711858

Other Books in the Current Controversies Series

Espionage
and Intelligence

Sylvia Engdahl, Book Editor

GREENHAVEN PRESS
A part of Gale, Cengage Learning

Detroit • New York • San Francisco • New Haven, Conn • Waterville, Maine • London

Elizabeth Des Chenes, *Director, Publishing Solutions*

For more information, contact:
Greenhaven Press
27500 Drake Rd.
Farmington Hills, MI 48331-3535
Or you can visit our Internet site at gale.cengage.com

For product information and technology assistance, contact us at

Gale Customer Support, 1-800-877-4253
For permission to use material from this text or product, submit all requests online at www.cengage.com/permissions

Further permissions questions can be emailed to permissionrequest@cengage.com

Articles in Greenhaven Press anthologies are often edited for length to meet page requirements. In addition, original titles of these works are changed to clearly present the main thesis and to explicitly indicate the author's opinion. Every effort is made to ensure that Greenhaven Press accurately reflects the original intent of the authors. Every effort has been made to trace the owners of copyrighted material.

Cover image © taelove7/Shutterstock.com.

LIBRARY OF CONGRESS CATALOGING-IN-PUBLICATION DATA

Espionage and intelligence / Sylvia Engdahl, book editor.
   p. cm. -- (Current controversies)
  Includes bibliographical references and index.
  ISBN 978-0-7377-5616-6 (hardcover) -- ISBN 978-0-7377-5617-3 (pbk.)
  1. National security--Law and legislation--United States. 2. Electronic surveillance--Law and legislation--United States. 3. Espionage--United States. 4. Intelligence service--Law and legislation--United States. I. Engdahl, Sylvia
  KF4850.E87 2012
  327.1273--dc23
                                              2012004310

Printed in the United States of America
1 2 3 4 5   16 15 14 13 12

ED150

Contents

Chapter 1: Is the Extent of American Espionage and Intelligence Gathering Necessary?

Yes: The Extent of Intelligence Gathering Is Necessary in Today's World

Although international espionage is associated by the public with the Cold War, it still exists. While today there is more tracking of terrorist activities than spying on governments, nations—even allies—spy on each other, and independent terrorist networks themselves are engaged in spying, as are major corporations that employ professional spies.

In 2011 the FBI's Next Generation Identification (NGI) system, the world's largest biometric database, became operational, and before long it will include facial recognition information and other biometric data as well as fingerprints. This and other agencies' databases will make it impossible for Americans to avoid scrutiny, which many believe violates their natural rights.

No: Intelligence Gathering on US Citizens Is Not Excessive

Chapter 3: How Is Technology Affecting Intelligence Gathering?

Not all the information obtained by intelligence agencies consists of stolen secrets. Much of it comes from sources open to anyone, such as the Internet and other forms of mass media. This does not mean that it is easy to decipher, for the intelligence officers who gather it must be fluent in foreign languages, familiar with foreign cultures, and experts in their fields of analysis.

Biometrics, the science of identifying people through their physical characteristics, has made great progress in recent years, but the problem of how best to use biometric data has yet to be solved. Privacy advocates object to the routine collection and storage of such data, and the government is attempting to work out effective ways of controlling access to it.

Valerie Caproni

The law requiring carriers to enable the government to intercept telecommunications was written at a time when the focus was on traditional telephone services rather than Internet services. As a result, the technical capability for intercepting many of today's most common communications is lacking.

William C. Banks

Technological changes in the way people communicate have made US laws controlling the interception of electronic communications by the government obsolete. Because the location of the parties has become meaningless, there is no way to avoid intercepting communications of innocent citizens. New laws to control the use of data, rather than its collection, are needed.

Chapter 4: Should Those Who Leak Government Secrets Be Prosecuted?

Josh Gerstein

Despite a campaign promise to conceal less from the public than past administrations have done, the Obama administration is prosecuting more federal workers who leak secret information than former administrations have. Intelligence officials argue that leaking is more harmful to national security than spying, but the conflict between secrecy and freedom of the press has created controversy.

Yes: Those Who Leak Government Secrets Should Be Prosecuted

No: Those Who Leak Secrets Should Not Be Prosecuted

The Espionage Act is an unconstitutional law that, if enforced, would apply to major newspapers, such as the *New York Times*, as much as it does to WikiLeaks. Many papers published information obtained from WikiLeaks, yet the government does not intend to prosecute them, which indicates that the attempt to bring charges against Julian Assange, WikiLeaks's founder, is not really about law enforcement but retribution.

Foreword

By definition, controversies are "discussions of questions in which opposing opinions clash" (Webster's Twentieth Century Dictionary Unabridged). Few would deny that controversies are a pervasive part of the human condition and exist on virtually every level of human enterprise. Controversies transpire between individuals and among groups, within nations and between nations. Controversies supply the grist necessary for progress by providing challenges and challengers to the status quo. They also create atmospheres where strife and warfare can flourish. A world without controversies would be a peaceful world; but it also would be, by and large, static and prosaic.

The Series' Purpose

The purpose of the Current Controversies series is to explore many of the social, political, and economic controversies dominating the national and international scenes today. Titles selected for inclusion in the series are highly focused and specific. For example, from the larger category of criminal justice, Current Controversies deals with specific topics such as police brutality, gun control, white collar crime, and others. The debates in Current Controversies also are presented in a useful, timeless fashion. Articles and book excerpts included in each title are selected if they contribute valuable, long-range ideas to the overall debate. And wherever possible, current information is enhanced with historical documents and other relevant materials. Thus, while individual titles are current in focus, every effort is made to ensure that they will not become quickly outdated. Books in the Current Controversies series will remain important resources for librarians, teachers, and students for many years.

In addition to keeping the titles focused and specific, great care is taken in the editorial format of each book in the series. Book introductions and chapter prefaces are offered to provide background material for readers. Chapters are organized around several key questions that are answered with diverse opinions representing all points on the political spectrum. Materials in each chapter include opinions in which authors clearly disagree as well as alternative opinions in which authors may agree on a broader issue but disagree on the possible solutions. In this way, the content of each volume in Current Controversies mirrors the mosaic of opinions encountered in society. Readers will quickly realize that there are many viable answers to these complex issues. By questioning each author's conclusions, students and casual readers can begin to develop the critical thinking skills so important to evaluating opinionated material.

Current Controversies is also ideal for controlled research. Each anthology in the series is composed of primary sources taken from a wide gamut of informational categories including periodicals, newspapers, books, U.S. and foreign government documents, and the publications of private and public organizations. Readers will find factual support for reports, debates, and research papers covering all areas of important issues. In addition, an annotated table of contents, an index, a book and periodical bibliography, and a list of organizations to contact are included in each book to expedite further research.

Perhaps more than ever before in history, people are confronted with diverse and contradictory information. During the Persian Gulf War, for example, the public was not only treated to minute-to-minute coverage of the war, it was also inundated with critiques of the coverage and countless analyses of the factors motivating U.S. involvement. Being able to sort through the plethora of opinions accompanying today's major issues, and to draw one's own conclusions, can be a complicated and frustrating struggle. It is the editors' hope that Current Controversies will help readers with this struggle.

Introduction

"A good deal of intelligence is derived from sources available to anyone."

Espionage has existed in every society since ancient times; groups, tribes, and nations have always spied on each other to learn what their enemies or rivals were doing or planning to do. But today, spying is involved in only a small fraction of intelligence operations. The American intelligence community consists of seventeen separate agencies and organizations, only a few of which are engaged in espionage, and a mere 5 percent of the intelligence they collect is obtained from secret sources.

Intelligence is a much broader term than *espionage*. Somewhat surprisingly, there is no generally accepted definition of it, although most people have a fairly good idea of what is meant by "intelligence agencies" and "intelligence gathering" and are aware these phrases cover far more than the stealing of secrets by spies. Intelligence is often defined as information, but obviously the term is limited to a specific kind of information. Michael Warner, in his article at the CIA's website titled "Wanted: A Definition of Intelligence," examines definitions proposed by many different writers and concludes that none of them are adequate. The one he himself proposes is: "Intelligence is secret, state activity to understand or influence foreign entities." The word is also, of course, used for the information acquired through that activity.

"The typical American, asked to define 'intelligence,'" Warner says, "is likely to evoke an image of some shadowy figure in a fedora and trenchcoat skulking in a dark alley. We intelligence officers know that stereotype is silly. . . . And yet the popular caricature possesses a certain wisdom, for it intuits that secrecy is a vital element—perhaps the key element—of intelligence." Whereas comparatively little of it is obtained from stolen secrets, much more of it is kept secret after it has been put together in a meaningful way. This is done by intelligence analysts, the vast majority of the men and women who work in the intelligence community whose job it is to correlate bits and pieces of data from various sources—data that may, when a pattern is seen, reveal something important. It is analysis that transforms information into intelligence. The significance of a particular fact is rarely known until it has been combined with other facts by someone with deep knowledge of the subject being investigated.

Thus a good deal of intelligence is derived from sources available to anyone—the media, websites, academic publications, and so forth. This is known as open source intelligence, or OSINT. Other major sources include intercepted communications (signals intelligence, or SIGINT); photographs, optical sensors, etc. (imagery intelligence, or IMINT); scientific data about the characteristics of targets (measurement and signature intelligence, or MASINT); and data from satellites, reconnaissance aircraft, etc. (geospatial intelligence, or GEOINT). Intelligence gained from human contacts—not only spies but diplomats, military attaches, foreign government officials, and even travelers—is called HUMINT.

There has always been a role for spies and there always will be, as long as nations have reason to distrust each other or fanatical groups arise within nations, but other forms of intelligence gathering now overshadow espionage. This is because of two recent developments that have changed both the work of intelligence agencies and the public's attitude toward them.

First, traditional espionage and intelligence gathering by governments was focused on learning the actions and plans of foreign governments. But today's greatest danger is from attack not by a foreign nation but by terrorists who act without their nation's official authorization. Moreover, not all the terrorists are outside America; some plan, and are likely to act, within its borders. To combat this threat it is necessary to gather intelligence about what is happening in the homeland as well as in foreign countries. And since without such intelligence it is impossible to determine which individuals are terrorists, this raises serious questions about the extent to which it is acceptable to gather information about innocent American citizens.

The second crucial development is the rapid advance of technology. People do not communicate in the same way they did even a few decades ago. Once, it could be assumed that enemies of America communicated mainly overseas and that Americans, with very few exceptions, did not. Geographic distinctions are meaningless today now that most communications occur via satellite and/or fiber-optic cable and both telephone and Internet traffic is routed far from the actual locations of the sender and receiver. Furthermore, the sheer volume of traffic has increased astronomically since the time when long-distance phone calling was an expensive luxury and the Internet did not exist.

At the same time, computers have provided a means of mass interception and recording of communication that would have been unimaginable during most of the twentieth century, as well a way of gaining fast access to information about individuals that would once have demanded days of work by a team of human investigators. Listening devices have been developed that not only facilitate the "bugging" of suspects, but that permit widespread surveillance of public places. Tracking devices—and even cell phones not in use—can reveal the movements of anyone authorities wish to follow.

Once, the use of these technologies by the government to keep tabs on people who have not been accused of any crime would have been considered entirely unacceptable, as they still are by a great many citizens. But after the terrorist attacks of

September 11, 2001, attitudes began to change. Laws were modified to allow intelligence agencies to do many things they had previously been barred from doing. There was fierce debate in Congress about some of these laws, and there were cases in which the president authorized tactics widely believed to be outside existing law entirely. These arguments are ongoing and will probably become even more heated as more and more invasive technologies are developed.

There is no easy resolution of the controversy. The invasion of citizens' privacy is contrary to America's fundamental ideals. Many people are outraged at the prospect of their personal data, such as physical characteristics, habits, and contacts, being stored in government computers, even though human analysts do not look at individual records unless there is some reason for suspicion. On the other hand, most also agree that they do not want any more people to be killed in terrorist attacks. If terrorists are allowed to infiltrate American society and operate in secret, then no one is safe. Some degree of surveillance is therefore essential in order to identify terrorists and find out what they are planning.

So the issue is where to draw the line—how to strike a balance between citizens' right to privacy and their right to be protected by the government from foreign-inspired violence. One guideline may lie in how surveillance data is used. Objections to its collection are often based less on the fact that this is being done than on the fear that once collected such data will be misused. Might the government start examining it for reasons other than identifying terrorists? Could there be a way to ensure that no future government will do so? Or does its very existence pose a danger that cannot be eliminated?

Questions like these will continue to be debated, and a balance of some sort between security and privacy will be maintained; but there will always be differences of opinion as to whether it is the right balance.

The viewpoints in *Current Controversies: Espionage and Intelligence* reflect the current debate on these topics, a debate likely to continue for some time as these thorny issues are slowly worked out on a policy level.

CHAPTER 1

Is the Extent of American Espionage and Intelligence Gathering Necessary?

Overview: The Mission of the US Intelligence Community

US Intelligence Community

The US Intelligence Community is a coalition of seventeen agencies and organizations within the executive branch of the US government.

The US Intelligence Community (IC) is a coalition of 17 agencies and organizations within the executive branch [of the US government] that work both independently and collaboratively to gather the intelligence necessary to conduct foreign relations and national security activities. Our primary mission is to collect and convey the essential information the President and members of the policymaking, law enforcement, and military communities require to execute their appointed duties.

The 17 IC member agencies are:

- Air Force Intelligence

- Army Intelligence

- Central Intelligence Agency

- Coast Guard Intelligence

- Defense Intelligence Agency

- Department of Energy

- Department of Homeland Security

- Department of State

- Department of the Treasury

"About the Intelligence Community," www.intelligence.gov, Office of the Director of National Intelligence. www.intelligence.gov, March 20, 2012.

- Drug Enforcement Administration

- Federal Bureau of Investigation

- Marine Corps Intelligence

- National Geospatial-Intelligence Agency

- National Reconnaissance Office

- National Security Agency

- Navy Intelligence

- Office of the Director of National Intelligence

Members of the IC collect and assess information regarding international terrorist and narcotic activities; other hostile activities by foreign powers, organizations, persons, and their agents; and foreign intelligence activities directed against the United States (U.S.). As needed, the President may also direct the IC to carry out special activities in order to protect U.S. security interests against foreign threats.

Threats Come in Many Forms

It used to be conventional military threats were all the United States had to worry about. Today, we live in a much more complex world where security concerns are less straightforward and susceptibility is more global in nature. The Intelligence Community (IC) now has to concern itself with:

Terrorism. Terrorism refers to premeditated, politically motivated violence against state or civilian targets carried out by subnational groups or clandestine agents intended as a protest or coercive act.

Proliferation. Proliferation is the conveyance of chemical, biological, radiological or nuclear weapons and/or technology by countries that possess them to ones that do not.

Chemical Warfare. Chemical warfare can be defined as the military use of chemicals, other than explosives, as weapons whose use results in incapacitation or death. It's the impact of a chemical's effect, instead of its physical effects, that distinguishes chemical weapons from conventional weapons.

Biological Warfare. Biological warfare is the deliberate use of pathogens or toxins for military or terrorist purposes. Biological warfare agents can be more toxic than chemical warfare nerve agents on a weight-for-weight basis and can potentially provide broader coverage per pound of payload. Biological warfare attacks can also be masked as naturally occurring epidemics due to the presence of a biological warfare agent such as *bacillus anthracis* (anthrax) in the environment.

Information Infrastructure Attack. Political activism on the Internet has generated a wide range of activity, from using e-mail and web sites to organize, to web page defacements and denial-of-service attacks. These computer-based attacks are usually referred to as hacktivism, a marriage of hacking and political activism.

Narcotics Trafficking. Along with prevention and treatment, law enforcement is essential for reducing drug use. Illegal drug trafficking inflicts violence and corruption on our communities. Law enforcement is the first line of defense against such unacceptable activity. In addition to federal investigative and enforcement efforts, IC member agencies are committed to support of local and state law enforcement in their efforts to combat illegal drug trafficking.

Counterintelligence. One responsibility of the IC is to identify, understand, prioritize and counteract the intelligence threats from foreign powers directed toward the United States. This activity is known as counterintelligence. Counterintelligence involves more than simply catching spies (counterespionage); it is concerned with understanding, and possibly neutralizing, all aspects of the foreign intelligence operations.

A Dynamic Process

Intelligence drives our national security policies, and the Intelligence Community is responsible for supplying accurate and usable information to those in charge of national security. The successful intelligence process converts acquired information into clear, comprehensible intelligence and delivers it to the President, policymakers, and military commanders in a form they can utilize to make educated policy decisions. Generating reliable, accurate intelligence is an active, never-ending process commonly referred to as the intelligence cycle.

The process begins with identifying the issues in which policy makers are interested and defining the answers they need to make educated decisions regarding those issues. We then lay out a plan for acquiring that information and go about collecting it. Once we have the proper intelligence, we sort through it, analyze what it means, and prepare summary reports and recommendations, which we deliver to national security policy makers. The answers our reports supply often reveal other areas of concern, which lead to more questions. In this way, the end of one cycle effectively leads to the start of the next. . . .

Information can be gathered from open, covert, electronic, and satellite sources.

During the management phase we determine what issues need to be addressed and what information must be gathered in order to provide the proper answers. We begin by examining finished intelligence from previous cycles, which leads us to formulate a strategic plan for new intelligence gathering and analysis. In this way, the end of one intelligence fuels another.

This stage depends on guidance from public officials. Policymakers, including the President, his aides, the National Security Council, and other major departments and agencies of government, initiate requests for intelligence. Issue coordinators from the Intelligence Community interact with these public officials to establish their core concerns and related information requirements. These needs then guide our collection strategies and allow us to produce the appropriate intelligence products.

Data Gathering

This stage, also known as collection, covers the acquisition of raw information through activities such as interviews, technical and physical surveillances, human source operation, searches, and liaison relationships. Information can be gathered from open, covert, electronic, and satellite sources.

There are six basic intelligence sources:

Signals Intelligence (SIGINT). The interception of signals, whether between people, between machines, or a combination of both.

The National Security Agency (NSA) is responsible for collecting, processing, and reporting SIGINT. Within the NSA, the National SIGINT Committee advises the Director, NSA, and the Director of National Intelligence (DNI) on policy issues and manages the SIGINT requirements system.

Imagery Intelligence (IMINT). Representations of objects reproduced electronically or by optical means on film, electronic display devices, or other media. It can be derived from visual photography, radar sensors, infrared sensors, lasers, and electro-optics.

The National Geospatial-Intelligence Agency manages all IMINT activities, both classified and unclassified, within the government. This includes requirements, collection, processing, exploitation, dissemination, archiving, and retrieval.

Measurement and Signature Intelligence (MASINT). Scientific and technical intelligence information used to locate, identify, or describe distinctive characteristics of specific targets. It employs a broad group of disciplines including nuclear, optical, radio frequency, acoustics, seismic, and materials sciences. For example, MASINT can identify distinctive radar signatures created by specific aircraft systems or the chemical composition of air and water samples.

The Central MASINT Organization, a component of the Defense Intelligence Agency, is the focus for all national and Department of Defense (DoD) MASINT matters.

Human-Source Intelligence (HUMINT). The oldest method for collecting information, this is intelligence derived from human sources. Collection includes clandestine acquisition of photography, documents, and other material; overt collection by personnel in diplomatic and consular posts; debriefing of foreign nationals and U.S. citizens who travel abroad; and official contacts with foreign governments. To the public, HUMINT is synonymous with espionage and clandestine activities. However, most of it is accumulated by overt collectors such as diplomats and military attaches.

HUMINT is used mainly by the Central Intelligence Agency (CIA), the Department of State (DoS), the DoD, and the FBI. The CIA, working closely with the Office of the Director of National Intelligence (ODNI) established the National Clandestine Service (NCS) to improve HUMINT throughout the IC. The NCS serves as the national authority for coordination, de-confliction, and evaluation of clandestine HUMINT operations, both abroad and inside the United States. While the ODNI establishes policy related to clandestine HUMINT, the NCS executes and implements that policy across the Intelligence Community (IC).

Open-Source Intelligence (OSINT). Publicly available information appearing in print or electronic form including radio, television, newspapers, journals, the Internet, commercial databases, and videos, graphics, and drawings.

While open-source collection responsibilities are broadly distributed through the IC, the major collectors of OSINT are the Foreign Broadcast Information Service and the National Air and Space Intelligence Center.

Geospatial Intelligence (GEOINT). Imagery and mapping data produced through an integration of imagery, imagery intelligence, and geospatial information. GEOINT is typically gathered from commercial satellites, government satellites, reconnaissance aircraft, or by other means such as maps, commercial databases, census information, GPS waypoints, utility schematics, or any discrete data that have locations on earth. This data is utilized to support our national security, which includes everything from assisting soldiers on the battlefield to assisting humanitarian and disaster relief efforts.

Interpretation, Analysis, and Reporting

The collection stage of the intelligence process typically yields large amounts of unfiltered data, which requires organization. Substantial U.S. intelligence resources are devoted to the synthesis of this data into a form intelligence analysts can use. Information filtering techniques include exploiting imagery; decoding messages and translating broadcasts; reducing telemetry to meaningful measures; preparing information for computer processing; storage and retrieval; and placing human-source reports into a form and context to make them more comprehensible.

Finished intelligence is hand-carried to the President and key national security advisers on a daily basis.

The fourth stage of the intelligence cycle involves converting basic information into finished documentation. This includes integrating, evaluating, and analyzing all available data—which is often fragmented and even contradictory—and distilling it into the final intelligence products, which highlight information on topics of immediate importance or make long-range assessments.

Analysts, who are subject-matter specialists, absorb incoming information, evaluate it, produce an assessment of the current state of affairs within an assigned field or substantive area, and then forecast future trends or outcomes. They integrate data into a coherent whole, put the evaluated information in context, and produce finished intelligence that includes assessments of events and judgments about the implications of the information for the United States (U.S.).

Analysts are encouraged to include alternative futures in their assessments and to look for opportunities to warn about possible developments abroad that could either provide threats to or opportunities for U.S. security and policy interests. Analysts also develop requirements for collection of new information.

Distribution

When information has been reviewed and correlated with data from other available sources, it is called finished intelligence, which is disseminated directly to the same policymakers whose initial needs generated the intelligence requirements. Finished intelligence is hand-carried to the President and key national security advisers on a daily basis. The policymakers then make decisions based on this information. These decisions may lead to requests for further examination, thus triggering the intelligence cycle one more time.

The Five Categories of Finished Intelligence:

- *Current Intelligence.* Addresses day-to-day events. It details new developments and related background in order to assess their significance, warn of their near-term consequences, and signal potentially dangerous situations in the near future.

- *Estimative Intelligence.* Looks forward to assess potential developments that could affect U.S. national security. By discussing the implications of a range of possible outcomes and alternative scenarios, estimative intelligence helps policymakers think strategically about long-term threats.

- *Warning Intelligence.* Sounds an alarm or gives notice to policymakers. It suggests urgency and implies the potential need to respond with policy action. Warning intelligence includes identifying or forecasting events that could cause the engagement of U.S. military forces, or those that would have a sudden and detrimental effect on U.S. foreign policy concerns such as coups, third-party wars, or refugee situations. Warning analysis involves exploring alternative futures and low probability/high impact scenarios.

- *Research Intelligence.* Research supports both current and estimative intelligence and is divided into two specialized subcategories: Basic intelligence primarily consists of the structured collection of geographic, demographic, social, military, and political data on foreign countries. Intelligence for operational support [is] tailored, focused, and rapidly produced intelligence for planners and operators that incorporates all types of intelligence production—current, estimative, warning, research, and scientific and technical.

- *Scientific and Technical Intelligence.* Includes an examination of the technical development, characteristics, performance, and capabilities of foreign technologies including weapon systems or subsystems. This covers a complete spectrum of sciences, technologies, weapon systems, and integrated operations.

Intelligence Gathering Is Necessary to Protect Against Terrorism

Richard J. Hughbank, Don Githens, and Robert D. Hughbank

Major Richard J. Hughbank, US Army (retired), is an assistant professor in the Criminal Justice Department at Northwestern State University teaching graduate homeland security studies. He is also the president of Extreme Terrorism Consulting, LLC. Hughbank, with over twenty-one years experience in the Military Police Corps, is a combat veteran in the War on Terror and a published author in the fields of security, active shooters, terrorism, and homeland security. Hughbank is currently a doctoral candidate in management and homeland security. He can be contacted through his company website www.understandterror .com, rhughbank@understandterror.com or on his professional blog on Facebook: "Understand Terror." Don Githens is a captain in the US Air Force with nine years experience as an intelligence officer and analyst. Robert (Bob) D. Hughbank is currently attending American Military University in the pursuit of an MA in homeland security. He is also the chief executive officer of Extreme Terrorism Consulting, LLC with over twenty years of experience in law enforcement, and was an intelligence analyst in the Army and a veteran of the Vietnam War. Bob is a published author in the fields of security, terrorism, and homeland security. He is certified by the Anti Terrorism Accreditation Board (ATAB) as a Certified Antiterrorist Specialist (CAS) and sits on the Terrorism Studies and Standards committee thereof. He can be contacted through his company website www.under standterror.com or rdhughbank@understandterror.com.

Richard J. Hughbank, Don Githens, and Robert D. Hughbank, "Intelligence and Its Role in Protecting Against Terrorism," *Journal of Strategic Security*, vol. 3, no. 1, 2010, pp. 31–36. Copyright © 2010 by Henly-Putnam University. All rights reserved. Reproduced by permission.

Intelligence is information that is analyzed and converted into a product to support a particular customer. Intelligence is both a process and a product and has played an important role in diplomacy and warfare throughout history. In the information age, intelligence has taken on an even greater importance. But in the popular media, the role, means, and purpose of intelligence is very often misrepresented at best. Only a tiny fraction of intelligence officers perform clandestine intelligence gathering. They don't assassinate people, carry weapons or even wear trench coats. The vast majority of the intelligence community carries out its mundane tasks at a computer terminal and, while intelligence alone cannot stop the next terrorist attack, it is *the* critical first step in identifying and possibly preventing one.

The art and science of gathering critical operational intelligence has been defined in many ways and is beyond our needs for this writing. Throughout the course of history, many wars have been fought depending heavily on various forms of intelligence. During our most recent actions in the War on Terror, intelligence analysis has played a critical role in both offensive and defensive operations in Iraq and Afghanistan. With such varying fact-finding techniques available and utilized in the defense of our country, it has become an arduous task to collect, decipher, package, prioritize, disseminate, and act upon everything that comes down the pipe.

Strategic intelligence is used for long-term planning and other broad topics such as operational capabilities of a potential opponent.

Intelligence is even more important in homeland defense and security. Our society is suspicious of intrusions on personal liberties. Mandated identity cards, restricted vehicle access and random searches of airline passengers are generally not well received. That makes it especially important to prevent terrorist attacks by interdicting the terrorists and their resources before they can reach their targets. The primary means of accomplishing this is through a combination of intelligence and law enforcement work.

Military intelligence branches have been extremely effective while operating in various countries with the use of multiple forms of intelligence: Human Intelligence (HUMINT), Geospatial Intelligence (GEOINT), Measurement and Signature Intelligence (MASINT), Open Source Intelligence (OSINT), Strategic Intelligence (STRATINT), Signals Intelligence (SIGINT), and Technical Intelligence (TECHINT). Simply stated, and reduced to the lowest common denominator, intelligence is information of the world about us. Regardless of the form of intelligence, the world can be divided into short-term, narrow focus, Tactical Intelligence, and long-term broad focus, Strategic Intelligence.

Strategic intelligence is used for long-term planning and other broad topics such as operational capabilities of a potential opponent and political assessments. With painstaking analysis and the use of computers to produce clear evaluations and concise intelligence assessments, local law enforcement can have a foundational tool to effectively use in an effort to identify potential terrorist operations and targets within their community. It's this functional ability to "predict" when and where future operational terrorist acts might occur and which tactical targets might prove more advantageous for a terrorist organization—whether it is psychological, economical, or political in nature—through the use of gathered and processed data from varying sources that places homeland defense in better offensive and defensive postures to successfully preempt and thwart their next attack.

Tactical Intelligence

Tactical intelligence is used for operational units and includes, among other things, human intelligence, open source intelligence, imagery intelligence, and direct observation. These particular sources require trained and dedicated street cops who can think on their feet and identify the simplest of cultural patterns and behavioral modifications of those who regularly work, play and live within their assigned patrol areas. In this age of technology, we have become so reliant upon computers that we've almost forgotten this most important point. For the remainder of this article, we will focus primarily on tactical intelligence and its critical role in identifying and defeating future terrorist acts in our communities.

Tactical intelligence is crucial in counterinsurgency and asymmetric warfare. Initiative and surprise can be achieved only if the tactical intelligence mission is effective. All possible vetted sources must be utilized to their optimal potential, including those frequently ignored. Therefore, a central clearinghouse should be established that collects and exploits all of the accumulated information then disseminates the assembled intelligence to the shift commanders so they can be passed on either at shift change or during the shift as deemed necessary. The officers in the street, in turn, need to pass on information gathered from their neighborhood sources to their designated information collector in a timely fashion. This is the only way the intelligence mission can have a chance of functioning at a level necessary to identify and possibly stop the next terrorist attack.

Intelligence Application

So, what exactly should you be searching for and passing on to the clearinghouse while patrolling and interacting with the neighborhood on an average shift? Well, you're looking for the same things you've been looking for since you left the academy; anything that's out of place or out of the ordinary; comments from the people on your beat that have a "strange" ring to them. You already know; anything that doesn't quite seem right to you through your training and experience on the street. New people in the neighborhood who avoid patrol cars, groups that break up when you slow down as you drive by, and different attitudes of people you've known over time are just some examples of things and acts to be watchful for. Those mundane reactive shifts *must* turn into proactive conversation and a critical eye for detail.

Having the ability to gain a sense of situational awareness for a certain area within a community will either deter or assist in gaining knowledge of "new" changes that directly impact the initial stages of terroristic-guerilla warfare in your assigned sectors. Remember, you're a trained observer; so observe and report accordingly.

The Army gets this right, as every soldier is a collector of information as part of their basic duties. No one particular unit or patrol is given the individual task of collecting and passing up [the chain of command] information while on patrol on any given mission and on varying degrees of terrain and areas of operation. Everyone receives an intelligence brief prior to beginning a mission or shift, and each individual is required to remain vigilant during their patrol with an additional requirement to continue gathering intelligence while out on the streets.

Intelligence is useless if it's inaccurate, or if it is presented in an unusable format when needed.

All police departments have the same potential—they rely on daily, personal interaction within their assigned sector of patrol to perform their duties. While the information they "collect" is for the purpose of protecting the populace, enforcing laws and preventing crime, some information can be useful to analysts tracking the potential terrorist threats within our borders. Almost every illegal activity can be given away by indicators. It's the observation of these indicators and the proper analysis of their significance that could directly lead to the defeat of future terrorist acts. Various stages of terrorist operations can be determined by the smallest of indicators provided during that particular operational maneuver. You won't necessarily recognize these indicators for what they are, but to an analyst who has studied a particular terrorist group or individual that indicator can speak volumes. The question is, how do you know what to look for?

In the intelligence community, the process of addressing this question is known as collection management. Analysts who study an intelligence problem (e.g., what are the plans and capabilities of a particular terrorist organization) have the best idea of what intelligence gaps exist. They identify these gaps to a collection manager (CM) in the form of a requirement. A requirement consists of priority and justification, essential elements of information and reporting requirements. The CM then integrates these requirements into a collection strategy. Finally, a collection plan is developed to detail a tactical level course of action and subsequently briefed to operators (e.g., SWAT [special weapons and tactics] and daily patrols) to carry out. The interaction of the analysts and collectors is absolutely essential to this entire process.

The Collection Cycle

As a process, intelligence is designed to support a person or organization. It is designed to assist decision makers, planners, operators and sometimes other intelligence organizations. Intelligence is useless if it's inaccurate, or if it is presented in an unusable format when needed. It's imperative the intelligence organization has a clear understanding of the tasking being levied. Tasking is the first step in the intelligence cycle (sometimes referred to as the collection cycle or TCPED [tasking, collection, processing, exploitation, and dissemination] cycle).

- *Tasking*: The tasking should originate with the person or organization being supported. The more involved the *customer* gets in tasking, and the more detailed that tasking is, the better the final product becomes. This tasking is referred to as a requirement, and it drives the rest of the collection cycle.

- *Collection*: This is the actual gathering of raw information. It can take the form of imagery (IMINT), a communications signal intercept (SIGINT), or a report from a person (HUMINT).

- *Processing*: This is the stage where raw data is converted to a useable format. SIGINT intercepts are translated, HUMINT reports are formatted and source information added, and IMINT is converted to customer specifications.

- *Exploitation*: Intelligence analysts analyze the information to determine its significance. The final product is created according to the customer's requirement at this stage.

- *Dissemination*: The finished intelligence product is delivered according to the customer's requirement.

The collection cycle for each intelligence discipline differs in timeliness and responsiveness. IMINT is probably the most timely and responsive, since technology allows for rapid processing and dissemination. IMINT is also active—an asset has to go out and take the pictures. SIGINT is not as timely, since signals usually need to be transcribed and/or translated. SIGINT technology is usually more sensitive, and thus access to the collected data is usually more restricted (classified). SIGINT also relies on the target being active in communication. HUMINT is usually the least timely, since collecting usually involves considerable risk to the person doing the collection. Security measures to ensure the safety of the collector definitely slow down the processing stage.

Fortunately, you don't need to be an expert on the capabilities of each intelligence discipline. The intelligence process is overseen by a collection manager (CM), an intelligence professional, usually experienced in a single intelligence discipline that helps the customer craft their requirement. The CM then determines the most effective intelligence discipline to satisfy the requirement, prioritizes it against other requirements, and tasks an intelligence resource to achieve the collection. A CM follows the requirement through the collection cycle, acting as an advocate for the customer.

Intelligence support can be a valuable tool to assist law enforcement agencies in the performance of their daily duties. It's especially relevant in counterterrorism investigations and operations. Terrorist organizations rely heavily on secrecy and anonymity to carry out their religious and politically driven agendas, and intelligence gathering and exploitation is best suited to stripping away this critical layer of protection and making them more vulnerable to infiltration, investigation and arrest. Intelligence work is a discipline in and of itself, just like police work, and carries its own language, rules, and culture. At times, it can be in direct conflict with law enforcement, but the goal of both remains the same; the protection of every American citizen and our way of life; our very culture, if you will.

Intelligence support can be . . . especially relevant in counterterrrosism investigations and operations.

As terrorism continues to plague the world through the global Salafi jihad movement [a violent Islamic movement], the United States will forever serve as a critical target for various organizations who seek to spread "pure" Islam. Through patience and vigilance, our enemies continue to further their cause through the understanding of our society. Thus, it becomes imperative we do the same. It is imperative we continue to learn about those who choose to attack our freedoms and way of life, and our law enforcement agencies will have to take the lead in this ongoing war. Indeed, the law enforcement community must develop transparent communication and intelligence links. While the days of fighting conventional crime are still at the forefront, our modern foes have defiantly presented us with a challenge that must be met with extreme prejudice if we are to successfully protect our nation and its citizens. The collection of intelligence will prove invaluable in this success, but we must learn to properly use this important tool at the strategic, operational, and tactical levels and it starts with training and utilizing every facet of our law enforcement agencies as they continue to patrol, and protect our neighborhoods.

Nations, Terrorist Organizations, and Major Corporations All Engage in Espionage

McKay Coppins

McKay Coppins is a reporter for Newsweek *and the Daily Beast website, covering politics, religion, and national affairs.*

The startling discovery of an undercover Russian spy ring last month [June 2010] no doubt shocked many Americans who assumed that international espionage was mostly a product of the Cold War and, these days, Hollywood.

But intelligence experts weren't the least surprised. "We forget that states like Russia have been conducting espionage for centuries," says Peter Earnest, a former member of the CIA who is now director of the Spy Museum in Washington, D.C. "It didn't stop with the Cold War and start again recently. It simply continued." Of course, diplomatic relations between the U.S. and Russia have improved in recent years, and Earnest says the two governments work together with an unspoken understanding that they are still spying on each other. "It's just the cost of doing business," he says.

While professional spying was once about nation-states looking over other governments' shoulders, today it's largely about tracking terrorists' activities and monitoring public communications for suspicious chatter. In fact, intelligence experts say espionage of all shades has actually increased since the Cold War, amplified by new technology and soaring demand for information in the public and private sectors. Just this week, *The Washington Post* reported that "some 1,271 government organizations and 1,931 private companies work on programs related to counterterrorism, homeland security, and intelligence in about 10,000 locations across the United States" as part of the paper's report on the top-secret world created by Washington after 9/11.

Here's a look at who's spying on whom, circa 2010:

Other Nations

When it comes to state-backed espionage, experts say the U.S. has focused much of its recent spying on Iran, North Korea, and China. And these countries, it appears, are returning the favor.

Earnest says the U.S. is the recipient of "hundreds of thousands" of cyberattacks every day, many of which emanate from Beijing. "They want to find out if they can penetrate our firewalls and actually learn intelligence. We believe a good deal has been learned."

But, of course, computers and satellites can do only so much. Secret agents, like the ones recently deported to Russia, still play a significant role in international spy games, though Earnest says the number of "illegals" currently undercover in the U.S. is unknowable. "The problem with counting spies is that [it is] their nature . . . not to be counted," he says.

Independent terror networks have proved adept at the art of deception and intelligence gathering.

Even longtime strong allies may spy on each other. An Israeli report in 2008 documented a long history of American spying on Israel, particularly in regard to Israel's secret nuclear program. And there have been several known instances of Israel spying on America, including the famous case of Jonathan Pollard, a U.S. intelligence analyst sentenced to life in prison after an espionage conviction.

Terrorists

Many Americans are under the false impression that "cave-dwelling terrorists" are too primitive to support effective intelligence operations, Earnest says. The most dangerous spies, however, are often the ones not working for recognized governments (which are bound, at least theoretically, by diplomacy and international law).

Independent terror networks have proved adept at the art of deception and intelligence gathering. The 2008 attack on Mumbai, [India,]says Earnest, "required a tremendous amount of planning as well as some relatively low-tech, but well-used, technology." And this January [2010], a double agent of [global terrorist network] Al Qaeda successfully infiltrated a CIA base in Afghanistan and killed seven agents in a suicide bombing, temporarily crippling America's intelligence operations in the country.

Major Corporations

Spying isn't just the stuff of war and international politics. While researching his 2010 book *Broker, Trader, Lawyer, Spy: The Secret World of Corporate Espionage,* journalist Eamon Javers uncovered the dealings of private-sector spy firms employed by companies to detect deception in negotiators, surveil competing investors, and glean intelligence that could give them an edge in their dealmaking. Espionage has become so ubiquitous in the corporate world, Javers says, that billion-dollar merger-and-acquisition deals are almost never made these days without highly skilled spies getting involved.

Using some of the most sophisticated technology in the world (like a laser that can record conversations from a kilometer away by picking up the slightest vibrations on an office window), these firms are staffed almost entirely by former military and intelligence officials, from the U.K.'s MI5 to Russia's KGB. The CIA even has a policy that allows its analysts to "moonlight" for major corporations. And there's no shortage of demand. One hedge-fund executive told Javers he used corporate spies to keep tabs on the entire board of directors for every company he invested in. "There is even a whole network of people who do nothing but track corporate jets," Javers says.

The advent of the Internet transformed the private-eye industry, shifting its focus from background checks . . . to surveillance.

It's not only competitors snooping around these major corporations. Both Earnest and Javers say foreign governments regularly spy on U.S. companies. "The Chinese have an extremely elaborate intelligence network aimed at penetrating defense and technology firms," Javers says. "Every piece of technology they steal is a piece they don't have to invent for themselves."

Private Investigators

The advent of the Internet transformed the private-eye industry, shifting its focus from background checks (which can now be completed for a small price on myriad Web sites) to surveillance.

Skipp Porteous, president of New York–based Sherlock Investigations, says much of his business is derived from spouses who suspect infidelity. "A lot of times we get calls from a wife whose husband is coming to New York, usually on business, and she's afraid he's going to fool around," Porteous says. "So she hires us and we get the goods." (Incidentally, Porteous says women are right in their suspicions about 90 percent of the time; when men think their wives are cheating, they're usually wrong.)

Sherlock dispatches teams of two licensed private investigators, experts at blending into crowds and going unnoticed, to follow the suspected cheater and snap photos. In one case, a woman from Bermuda hired Sherlock to follow her husband while he was in New York. Investigators took pictures of him with six prostitutes (at once) and e-mailed them to their client before her spouse returned home.

Additionally, since the Internet has enabled people to easily purchase illegal audio and video transmitters, Sherlock has seen a boom in "bug sweep" business, especially among celebrities who believe the paparazzi have infiltrated their homes or cars. As new technologies emerge, experts expect intelligence and counterintelligence methods to grow in sophistication, and generate even more job opportunities for a new generation of supersleuths.

National Security Needs Justify Deceptive Recruitment of Spies

David L. Perry

David L. Perry is the director of the Vann Center for Ethics at Davidson College in North Carolina.

When the CIA is unable to obtain voluntary agents, it sometimes "recruits" them, so to speak, through *deception*. In some cases, people who wouldn't willingly work for the CIA are made unwittingly to do exactly that by passing information to a trusted friend or associate who happens to be in the CIA employ but who presents himself as one with loyalties more congenial to the person being duped. This method is sometimes called "false-flag" recruitment, since the recruiter claimed to be someone he's not. It's essentially a con game, wherein one first ascertains the potential agent's basic loyalties and core values to concoct a scheme to persuade him to provide sensitive information without upsetting his conscience or arousing his suspicions.

In his book published during the Cold War, Miles Copeland suggested that "[i]f the prospective agent hates Americans," for example, the recruiter "can tell him he is acting on behalf of the French—or the British, the Soviets, or some senator or crusading newspaperman," whatever his conscience is assessed as most likely to tolerate. David Phillips, another former CIA officer, attested that "there are unsuspecting zealots around the world who are managed and paid as spies; they sell their countries' secrets believing all the while they are helping 'the good guys.'" Note that one's opponent can also play this game; Phillips continued:

David L. Perry, *Partly Cloudy: Ethics in War, Espionage, Covert Action and Interrogation*, MD: Scarecrow Press, 2009, pp. 139–140, 152–154. Copyright © 2009 by David L. Perry. All rights reserved. Reproduced by permission.

A Soviet KGB officer . . . might pose as a right-wing American in approaching a conservative U.S. government employee. He would attempt to persuade the American to report on the inner workings of his agency or department "to help my patriotic organization to be sure the Commies aren't infiltrating our institutions."

Former CIA counterintelligence officer William Johnson described another example of deceptive recruitment:

Once . . . we found the KGB using a false Israeli flag; that is, pretending to represent the Israeli Service in recruiting Jewish refugees who had access to Allied secrets. At first, the recruited agents were asked to provide information from Allied files on Nazi war criminals, and then they were blackmailed to give Allied military information.

A false-flag recruitment is odd from a moral perspective, since in one respect the agents willingly provide sensitive information, probably knowing that they would be punished if their activities were exposed, but of course the voluntary nature of such an action is only superficial, since if the agents knew to whom the information was actually being passed, they would most likely not provide it. . . .

Agents usually deserve not to be deceived about the risks involved in the operations they are asked to carry out, nor should the fact that their work is secret tempt their handlers to treat them as expendable.

Agents Treated as Expendable

The use of human agents—voluntary and nonvoluntary—is intended to provide information believed to be unobtainable through other methods. The risks inherent in all espionage activities suggest, though, that for the sake of the agent alone, efforts should be made to determine before the agent is recruited that the information needed cannot be ascertained by less problematic methods. In addition, since after an agent is recruited the agent-officer relationship takes on a life and momentum of its own, care must be taken to avoid situations where innocent third parties would be harmed or justice obstructed in the interest of preserving the agent's identity and continued service.

Recruiting voluntary agents has the advantage of involving no deception about the identity and general motives of the recruiter. Furthermore, a just cause can be served by intelligence officers and voluntary agents working together to undermine an unjust regime, but such agents usually deserve not to be deceived about the risks involved in the operations they are asked to carry out, nor should the fact that their work is secret tempt their handlers to treat them as expendable, to allow them to be callously sacrificed to Realpolitik [merely practical political ends] or the shifting winds of diplomacy.

The chief advantage of employing a false-flag approach or blackmail in certain situations is that intelligence gathering objectives can be pursued even where foreign citizens are highly unlikely to voluntarily serve as CIA agents, but such methods raise very difficult ethical questions. False-flag methods by definition deceive the agent as to the identity of the recruiter, and thus hide from the agent the full risks inherent in his or her tasks as well as their true purposes. Blackmail is blatant coercion. It is difficult enough to justify its use against known criminals; all the more so when it arises out of the calculated entrapment of a previously innocent person who merely happens to have probable access to sensitive information desired by the CIA. Finally, to the extent that false-flag and blackmail tactics seek to "stretch" the agent's conscience, they can result in the corruption of the agent in addition to his or her victimization.

When Deception Is Justified

The primarily deontological [morally obligatory] concerns about espionage are challenged, though, by the consequentialist [one who values ends over means] reply that if one rules out an espionage source or method, one may thereby eliminate the possibility of knowing certain kinds of vital information. It's not difficult to construct hypothetical cases in which having particular information about the intentions of a tyrannical regime or a terrorist cell could mean the difference between life and death for many people, cases that would therefore question the validity of strict prohibitions on deceptive and coercive intelligence methods or the use of criminals as agents.

Clandestine collection of intelligence using human agents will remain vital in penetrating hostile intelligence agencies (counterespionage); in monitoring the existence, movements, proliferation, and elimination of weapons of mass destruction; and in monitoring and subverting international terrorism and narcotics trafficking.

The examination of Soviet tactics . . . for example, suggests the broad outline of an argument for a just cause undergirding U.S. espionage capabilities. Even if the role of state security in Soviet history and external affairs is downplayed, the military threat posed by the Soviet Union after World War II would have been enough by itself to warrant the development of a global U.S. clandestine intelligence collection capability, supplemented by intelligence liaison with allied governments to expose and expel Soviet spies.

The Soviet case is admittedly anomalous in the sense that no other country has posed the same sort of threat to the United States in degree or scope, but a generalization can legitimately be made from the Soviet case to justify U.S. espionage efforts against other countries and organizations similarly antagonistic toward liberal democracy. Clandestine collection of intelligence using human agents will remain vital in penetrating hostile intelligence agencies (counterespionage); in monitoring the existence, movements, proliferation, and elimination of weapons of mass destruction; and in monitoring and subverting international terrorism and narcotics trafficking.

An additional point needs to be made, however, concerning the meaning of moral justification in the present context. To say that a decision or action is morally justified does mean that is the right or best decision or action all things considered, but it does not necessarily mean that the outcome from such a decision is unequivocally good. It may be, for example, that coercive recruitment of an agent can be morally justified in a particular situation (given the dire consequences of not having the information that he or she can provide, say, plus a lack of morally acceptable alternatives), but since coercion involves an infringement of the agent's freedom (and conceivably other basic rights), the external good that may result from the recruitment cannot do away with the fact that the agent—an autonomous human being with values, emotions, hopes, and dreams, who is not merely an abstract "source," "asset," or "penetration"—suffers real harm in the process. This recognition at least ought to have a sobering effect on the consideration of the ends of U.S. espionage and covert action. If national security can justify the coercive recruitment of agents, it is not clear that lesser ends can.

Harsh Interrogation Methods Are a Necessary Means of Combating Terrorism

Michael B. Mukasey

Michael B. Mukasey, a lawyer and former judge, was the attorney general of the United States from 2007 to 2009.

Osama bin Laden [the leader of al Qaeda terrorist network] was killed by Americans, based on intelligence developed by Americans. That should bring great satisfaction to our citizens and elicit praise for our intelligence community. Seized along with bin Laden's corpse was a trove of documents and electronic devices that should yield intelligence that could help us capture or kill other terrorists and further degrade the capabilities of those who remain at large.

But policies put in place by the very administration that presided over this splendid success promise fewer such successes in the future. Those policies make it unlikely that we'll be able to get information from those whose identities are disclosed by the material seized from bin Laden. The administration also hounds our intelligence gatherers in ways that can only demoralize them.

Finding bin Laden

Consider how the intelligence that led to bin Laden came to hand. It began with a disclosure from Khalid Sheikh Mohammed (KSM), who broke like a dam under the pressure of harsh interrogation techniques that included waterboarding. He loosed a torrent of information—including eventually the nickname of a trusted courier of bin Laden.

Michael B. Mukasey, "The Waterboarding Trail to Bin Laden," *Wall Street Journal*, May 6, 2011. Copyright © 2011 by Dow Jones & Company. All rights reserved. Reproduced by permission.

That regimen of harsh interrogation was used on KSM after another detainee, Abu Zubaydeh, was subjected to the same techniques. When he broke, he said that he and other members of al Qaeda were obligated to resist only until they could no longer do so, at which point it became permissible for them to yield. "Do this for all the brothers," he advised his interrogators.

As late as 2006 . . . fully half of the government's knowledge about the structure and activities of al Qaeda came from [harsh] interrogations.

Abu Zubaydeh was coerced into disclosing information that led to the capture of Ramzi bin al Shibh, another of the planners of 9/11. Bin al Shibh disclosed information that, when combined with what was learned from Abu Zubaydeh, helped lead to the capture of KSM and other senior terrorists and the disruption of follow-on plots aimed at both Europe and the United States.

Another of those gathered up later in this harvest, Abu Haraj al-Libi, also was subjected to certain of these harsh techniques and disclosed further details about bin Laden's couriers that helped in last weekend's achievement [the elimination of bin Laden in early May 2011].

The harsh techniques themselves were used selectively against only a small number of hard-core prisoners who successfully resisted other forms of interrogation, and then only with the explicit authorization of the director of the CIA. Of the thousands of unlawful combatants captured by the U.S., fewer than 100 were detained and questioned in the CIA program. Of those, fewer than one-third were subjected to any of these techniques.

Former CIA Director Michael Hayden has said that, as late as 2006, even with the growing success of other intelligence tools, fully half of the government's knowledge about the structure and activities of al Qaeda came from those interrogations. The [George W.] Bush administration put these techniques in place only after rigorous analysis by the Justice Department, which concluded that they were lawful. Regrettably, that same administration gave them a name—"enhanced interrogation techniques"—so absurdly antiseptic as to imply that it must conceal something unlawful.

Banning Harsh Techniques

The current president [Barack Obama] ran for election on the promise to do away with them even before he became aware, if he ever did, of what they were. Days after taking office he directed that the CIA interrogation program be done away with entirely, and that interrogation be limited to the techniques set forth in the Army Field Manual, a document designed for use by even the least experienced troops. It's available on the Internet and used by terrorists as a training manual for resisting interrogation.

In April 2009, the administration made public the previously classified Justice Department memoranda analyzing the harsh techniques, thereby disclosing them to our enemies and assuring that they could never be used effectively again. Meanwhile, the administration announced its intentions to replace the CIA interrogation program with one administered by the FBI. In December 2009, Omar Faruq Abdulmutallab was caught in an airplane over Detroit trying to detonate a bomb concealed in his underwear. He was warned after apprehension of his Miranda rights [constitutional rights explained to every arrestee], and it was later disclosed that no one had yet gotten around to implementing the new program.

Yet the Justice Department, revealing its priorities, had gotten around to reopening investigations into the conduct of a half-dozen CIA employees alleged to have used undue force against suspected terrorists. I say "reopening" advisedly because those investigations had all been formally closed by the end of 2007, with detailed memoranda prepared by career Justice Department prosecutors explaining why no charges were warranted. Attorney General Eric Holder conceded that he had ordered the investigations reopened in September 2009 without reading those memoranda. The investigations have now dragged on for years with prosecutors chasing allegations down rabbit holes, with the CIA along with the rest of the intelligence community left demoralized.

Immediately following the killing of bin Laden, the issue of interrogation techniques became in some quarters the "dirty little secret" of the event. But as disclosed in the declassified memos in 2009, the techniques are neither dirty nor, as noted by Director Hayden and others, were their results little. As the memoranda concluded—and as I concluded reading them at the beginning of my tenure as attorney general in 2007—the techniques were entirely lawful as the law stood at the time the memos were written, and the disclosures they elicited were enormously important. That they are no longer secret is deeply regrettable.

We ... need to put an end to the ongoing investigations of CIA operatives that continue to undermine intelligence community morale.

It is debatable whether the same techniques would be lawful under statutes passed in 2005 and 2006—phrased in highly abstract terms such as "cruel, inhuman and degrading" treatment—that some claimed were intended to ban waterboarding even though the Senate twice voted down proposals to ban the technique specifically. It is, however, certain that intelligence-gathering rather than prosecution must be the first priority, and that we need a classified interrogation program administered by the agency best equipped to administer it: the CIA.

We also need to put an end to the ongoing investigations of CIA operatives that continue to undermine intelligence community morale.

Acknowledging and meeting the need for an effective and lawful interrogation program, which we once had, and freeing CIA operatives and others to administer it under congressional oversight, would be a fitting way to mark the demise of Osama bin Laden.

US Intelligence Operations Are Hindered by Competition Among Agencies

Ron Capps

Ron Capps was director of human intelligence and counterintelligence operations for US forces in Afghanistan in 2002 and 2003 and division chief in the State Department's Bureau of Intelligence and Research from 2006 to 2008.

In recent weeks, following the shocks of the Christmas Day bomber and the Dec. 30 [2009] attack on a U.S. base in Afghanistan, observers have tried to understand why U.S. intelligence failed so badly. President Barack Obama argued that the intelligence-gatherers have been doing a bang-up job, while the analysts back at home have not. The Christmas attack, he said, was "a failure to integrate and understand the intelligence that we already had." Then a *New York Times* article asserted that the problem is really communication between different sectors. Finally, the senior U.S. military intelligence officer in Afghanistan, Maj. Gen. Michael Flynn, blasted intelligence-gathering in Afghanistan, calling data "only marginally relevant" because it was disconnected from local politics and conditions on the ground.

But any evaluation that merely blames the analysts, the intelligence-gatherers, or even both of their abilities to communicate misses the point: Major parts of the system itself are broken, and no surface-level changes will fix that.

The trouble starts with bias. I spent a few years working in the field as an intelligence collector, a few more directing operations, and a few back in Washington as an analyst and manager. Like everyone else in the business, I have preferences for certain ways of collecting information. But part of the reason that U.S. intelligence has so much difficulty catching terrorists and quashing insurgencies is that these biases aren't just individual—they are corporate.

Competition Among Agencies

Within the intelligence community there are numerous collection methods known to insiders as "ints": satellite imagery (imint), electronic eavesdropping (sigint), human sources (humint), and so on. Each of these ints has a value and a purpose. But senior managers, analysts, and operators within the alphabet soup of no less than 16 agencies tasked with mastering these methods tend to become so deeply entrenched in the arcana [secrets] of their own fields that they can fail to appreciate the products of their colleagues.

Agencies and collectors each develop their separate little fiefdoms. And inevitably, competition results.

Consumers of the intelligence also have their favorites. Special Forces operators love imagery. Navy guys get really excited over electronic intelligence. Consumers develop a relationship with a collector and the analysts in that field and then start to lobby for that specialty, urging Congress to pour money into the so-called "black" budgets—the sections that don't appear on the regular, unclassified version.

Little by little, agencies and collectors each develop their separate little fiefdoms. And inevitably, competition results. Agencies vie for the ear of senior leaders, most importantly the president. The objective is to be the indispensable agency, the one that fills the pages of the President's Daily Brief (or simply PDB, as insiders call it). The competition drives arrogance and a lack of trust and respect among agencies. As an analyst and a manager of analysts, my biggest problem was getting other agencies to tell me what they knew. When advising policy designers and decision makers, I was often forced to answer their queries with "I don't know; Langley [CIA headquarters] won't tell us."

And the competition doesn't end there. Funding is another sought-after prize that erects dangerous barriers between all the agencies fighting for it. Technology can also prove a problem. For example, intelligence-system designers create unique hardware platforms and software applications for each agency, and sometimes for separate elements within agencies. Because each of these platforms and applications requires hard firewalls, gaps can occur, and agencies or sections of agencies can get shut out of intelligence-sharing.

Take the case of the newest military command, Africom. To build its intelligence database, analysts and managers had to collect data from the three major commands that were previously responsible for watching the African continent. Each command had used different and incompatible data storage software, making it nearly impossible for the data to be collated. The lines are drawn even more impenetrably between the foreign intelligence services (think CIA and the Defense Intelligence Agency) and the domestic law-enforcement communities (think FBI and the Department of Homeland Security). Now, imagine being an analyst at the National Counterterrorism Center, intended to pool and analyze all that data. Senior managers might have four or five different computer hard drives at their desks in order to access upward of 20 different intranets.

Secrecy for Its Own Sake

If you think that's bad, here's another barrier to intelligence-sharing: the love of secrecy for its own sake. Information is categorized and classified into levels from Confidential to Top Secret according to the level of damage to the United States its disclosure might cause. Information can be even further caveated so that, say, among Top Secret analysts, only certain analysts and consumers can view it. All this is meant to protect not only the information but where it came from and how it was collected, the sources and methods used. And in principle, of course, it is correct and necessary. In reality, such categorizations stovepipe information, and they are often used irresponsibly.

The big-brain analysts in Washington classify their work at such a level that information cannot be sent forward to troops in the field.

Such problems are hardly new. During the Vietnam War, combat commanders complained that their intelligence officers didn't share critical information with them. When I was a young intelligence officer, this was referred to as "green door syndrome" for the literal closed door behind which we worked.

Today, the door is electronic but just as effective. Commanders in the field have all the requisite clearances to know what sigint or humint is bringing in, but the big-brain analysts in Washington classify their work at such a level that information cannot be sent forward to troops in the field—who are, ironically, some of those who collected the raw data in the first place.

Flynn says he's going to set up offices in Afghanistan where anyone with something to share or who needs information can come and talk to an analyst. He's on to something. Probably 90 percent of what we need to know is unclassified. Known in the community as open-source material, it's the stuff that's in newspapers, on the radio, stuffed in some professor's head, or happening on the street to be observed. The remaining 10 percent is stuff that's really hard to get, and that's what our intelligence services go after.

So what's the solution? Publishing more reports unclassified would be a start. I once tried to publish a piece this way. I had written it based on information I collected myself in the field, and I wanted anyone who needed it to be able to access it easily. But the mere idea of my organization publishing something unclassified was so foreign that it took three weeks to get it cleared—that's about 2 1/2 weeks longer than usual. In some organizations, the format of their reports is considered confidential, so regardless of the source, even if it's a local newspaper, the report itself is classified.

These are the true failings that Obama described last week. It's up to him and to the director of national intelligence, Dennis Blair, to resolve them and to rethink the system itself. Until that happens, in Afghanistan, in the Horn of Africa, and in other places where what we don't know really can hurt us, we'll continue fighting ourselves as well as our enemies.

Brutal Methods of Interrogation Are Unjustifiable Even If Effective

Glenn Greenwald

Glenn Greenwald, a lawyer and award-winning journalist, writes a blog for the online magazine Salon. *He is also the author of several best-selling books.*

The killing of Osama bin Laden has, as the *New York Times* notes, reignited the debate over "brutal interrogations"—by which it's meant that Republicans are now attempting to exploit the emotions generated by the killing to retroactively justify the torture regime they implemented. The factual assertions on which this attempt is based—that waterboarding and other "harsh interrogation methods" produced evidence crucial to locating bin Laden—are dubious in the extreme. . . . So fictitious are these claims that even [former secretary of defense] Donald Rumsfeld has repudiated them.

But even if it were the case that valuable information were obtained during or after the use of torture, what would it prove? Nobody has ever argued that brutality will never produce truthful answers. It is sometimes the case that if you torture someone long and mercilessly enough, they will tell you something you want to know. Nobody has ever denied that. In terms of the tactical aspect of the torture debate, the point has always been—as a consensus of interrogations professionals has repeatedly said—that there are far more effective ways to extract the truth from someone than by torturing it out of them. The fact that one can point to an instance where torture produced the desired answer proves nothing about whether there were more effective ways of obtaining it.

A Glaring Fallacy

This highlights what has long been a glaring fallacy in many debates over War on Terror policies: that Information X was obtained after using Policy A does not prove that Policy A was necessary or effective. That's just basic logic. This fallacy asserted itself constantly in the debate over warrantless surveillance. Proponents of the Bush NSA [National Security Agency] program would point to some piece of intelligence allegedly obtained during warrantless eavesdropping as proof that the illegal program was necessary and effective; obviously, though, that fact said nothing about whether the same information would also have been discovered through legal eavesdropping, i.e., eavesdropping approved in advance by the FISA [Foreign Intelligence Surveillance Act] court (and indeed, legal eavesdropping [like legal interrogation tactics] is typically more effective than the illegal version because, by necessity, it is far more focused on actual suspected Terrorism plots; warrantless eavesdropping entails the unconstrained power to listen in on any communications the Government wants without having to establish its connection to terrorism). But in all cases, the fact that some piece of intelligence was obtained by some lawless Bush/Cheney War on Terror policy (whether it be torture or warrantless eavesdropping) proves nothing about whether that policy was effective or necessary.

> *There are many actions that the U.S. could take that would advance its interests that are nonetheless obviously wrong on moral and legal grounds.*

And those causal issues are, of course, entirely independent of the legal and moral questions shunted to the side by this reignited "debate." There are many actions that the U.S. could take that would advance its interests that are nonetheless obviously wrong on moral and legal grounds. When [business magnate] Donald Trump recently suggested that we should simply take Libya's oil and that of any other country which we successfully invade and occupy, that suggestion prompted widespread mockery. That was the reaction despite the fact that stealing other countries' oil would in fact produce substantial benefits for the U.S. and advance our interests: it would help to lower gas prices, reduce our dependence on hostile oil-producing nations, and avoid having to degrade our own environment in order to drill domestically. Trump's proposal is morally reprehensible and flagrantly lawless despite how many benefits it would produce; therefore, no person of even minimal decency would embrace it no matter how many benefits it produces.

Exactly the same is true for the torture techniques used by the Bush administration and once again being heralded by its followers (and implicitly glorified by media stars who keep suggesting that they enabled bin Laden's detection). It makes no difference whether it extracted usable intelligence. Criminal, morally depraved acts don't become retroactively justified by pointing to the bounty they produced.

CHAPTER 2

Is Too Much Intelligence Being Gathered on US Citizens?

Overview: New Monitoring Technologies Are Used for Surveillance of Average Citizens

Activist Post

Activist Post *is an independent news blog for activists challenging abuses by the establishment.*

The war on terror is a worldwide endeavor that has spurred massive investment into the global surveillance industry—which now seems to be becoming a war on "liberty and privacy." Given all of the new monitoring technology being implemented, the uproar over warrantless wiretaps now seems moot. High-tech, first-world countries are being *tracked, traced, and databased*, literally around every corner. Governments, aided by private companies, are gathering a mountain of information on average citizens who so far seem willing to trade liberty for supposed security. Here are just some of the ways the matrix of data is being collected:

- *GPS*—Global positioning chips are now appearing in everything from U.S. passports, cell phones, to cars. More common uses include tracking employees, and for all forms of private investigation. Apple recently announced they are collecting the precise location of iPhone users via GPS for public viewing in addition to spying on users in other ways.

- *Internet*—Internet browsers are recording your every move forming detailed cookies on your activities. The NSA [National Security Agency] has been exposed as having cookies on their site that don't expire until 2035. Major search engines know where you surfed last summer, and online purchases are databased, supposedly for advertising and customer service uses. IP [Internet protocol] addresses are collected and even made public. Controversial websites can be flagged internally by government sites, as well as re-routing all traffic to block sites the government wants to censor. It has now been fully admitted that social networks provide NO privacy to users, while technologies for real-time social network monitoring are already being used. The Cybersecurity Act attempts to legalize the collection and exploitation of your personal information. Apple's iPhone also has browsing data recorded and stored. All of this despite the overwhelming opposition to cybersurveillance by citizens.

- *RFID* [radio-frequency identification]—Forget your credit cards, which are meticulously tracked, or the membership cards for things so insignificant as movie rentals which require your SSN [Social Security Number]. Everyone has Costco, CVS, grocery-chain cards, and a wallet or purse full of many more. RFID "proximity cards" take tracking to a new level in uses ranging from loyalty cards, student ID, physical access, and computer network access. Latest developments include an RFID powder developed by Hitachi, for which the multitude of uses are endless—perhaps including tracking hard currency so we can't even keep cash undetected. (Also see microchips below).

- *Traffic cameras*—License plate recognition has been used to remotely automate duties of the traffic police in the United States, but have been proven to have dual use in England such as to mark activists under the Terrorism Act. Perhaps the most common use will be to raise money and shore up budget deficits via traffic violations, but uses may descend to such "Big Brother" tactics as monitors telling pedestrians not to litter as talking cameras already do in the UK.

- *Computer cameras and microphones*—The fact that laptops—contributed by taxpayers—spied on public school children (at home) is outrageous. Years ago Google began officially to use computer "audio fingerprinting" for advertising uses. They have admitted to working with the NSA, the premier surveillance network in the world. Private communications companies already have been exposed routing communications to the NSA. Now, keyword tools—typed and spoken—link to the global security matrix.

- *Public sound surveillance*—This technology has come a long way from only being able to detect gunshots in public areas, to now listening in to whispers for dangerous "keywords." This technology has been launched in Europe to "monitor conversations" to detect "verbal aggression" in public places. Sound Intelligence is the manufacturer of technology to analyze speech, and their website touts how it can easily be integrated into other systems.

- *Biometrics*—The most popular biometric authentication scheme employed for the last few years has been Iris Recognition. The main applications are entry control, ATMs and Government programs. Recently, network companies and governments have utilized biometric authentication including fingerprint analysis, iris recognition, voice recognition, or combinations of these for use in National identification cards.

- *DNA*—DNA blood from babies has been taken for all people under the age of 38. In England, DNA was sent to secret databases from routine heel prick tests. Several reports have revealed covert Pentagon databases of DNA for "terrorists" and now DNA from all American citizens is databased. Digital DNA is now being used as well to combat hackers.

- *Microchips*—Microsoft's HealthVault and VeriMed partnership is to create RFID implantable microchips. Microchips for tracking our precious pets is becoming commonplace and serves to condition us to accept putting them in our children in the future. The FDA [Food and Drug Administration] has already approved this technology for humans and is marketing it as a medical miracle, again for our safety.

- *Facial recognition*—Anonymity in public is over. Admittedly used at Obama's campaign events, sporting events, and most recently at the G8/G20 [economic summit] protests in Canada. This technology is also harvesting data from Facebook images and surely will be tied into the street "traffic" cameras.

It is not enough to have logged and charted where we have been; the surveillance state wants to know where we are going.

All of this is leading to *Predictive Behavior Technology*—It is not enough to have logged and charted where we have been; the surveillance state wants to know where we are going through psychological profiling. It's been marketed for such uses as blocking hackers. Things seem to have advanced to a point where a truly scientific Orwellian world is at hand. It is estimated that computers know to a 93% accuracy where you will be, before you make your first move. Nanotech is slated to play a big role in going even further as scientists are using nanoparticles to directly influence behavior and decision making.

Many of us are asking: What would someone do with all of this information to keep us tracked, traced, and databased? It seems the designers have no regard for the right to privacy and desire to become the Controllers of us all.

Warrantless Review of Americans' Everyday Communications Violates Constitutional Rights

Cindy Cohn

Cindy Cohn is the legal director of the Electronic Frontier Foundation. She has been named by the National Law Journal *as one of the fifty most influential women lawyers in America.*

Both former NSA [National Security Agency] Director Michael Hayden and former Justice Department attorney John Yoo have taken to the editorial pages of major national newspapers this summer [2009] to defend the so-called Presidential Surveillance Program, the still-shadowy set of programs that spy on Americans in America without any probable cause or warrant. This campaign to sway public opinion is ongoing because neither the past [George W.] Bush officials nor the current [Barack] Obama administration officials dare to defend their illegal activities on the merits in a court of law.

While the details are unknown, credible evidence indicates that billions of everyday communications of ordinary Americans are swept up by government computers and run through a process that includes both data-mining and review of content, to try to figure out whether any of us were involved in illegal or terrorist-related activity. That means that even the most personal and private of our electronic communications—between doctors and patients, between husbands and wives, or between children and parents—are subject to review by computer algorithms programmed by government bureaucrats or by the bureaucrats themselves.

It's a bizarre turn of events, these unwarranted general searches. Our country was founded on the rejection of "general warrants"—pieces of paper that gave the Executive (then the King) unchecked power to search colonial Americans without cause. The Fourth Amendment was adopted in part to stop these "hated writs" and to make sure that searches of the papers of Americans required a probable cause showing to a court. The warrantless surveillance program returns us to the policies of King George III, only with a digital boost. It subjects a huge number of our daily digital papers to threshold surveillance, then adding subsequent, more intrusive warrantless surveillance if faceless government computers and bureaucrats determine that our communications or communication patterns merit further scrutiny.

What [government] officials call a "gap" between domestic surveillance authority and our ability to conduct surveillance of foreigners abroad is where our constitutional rights reside.

Unconstitutional Surveillance

Both Yoo and Hayden draw from a similar bag of tricks to defend the surveillance programs, including claims that there was a "gap" between our domestic surveillance and our foreign intelligence surveillance.

They also cite the briefings given to select members of Congress, which the members themselves say were often incomplete and even possibly misleading. They then rely on the fact that hand-picked Bush administration political appointee attorneys signed off. But all of these rationales dodge the critical constitutional questions raised by wholesale surveillance of Americans without probable cause or a judicial determination. What these Bush officials call a "gap" between domestic surveillance authority and our ability to conduct surveillance of foreigners abroad is where our constitutional rights reside.

The Bush administration's central view was that the executive branch was somehow above the niceties of the Constitution. What's clear now, and deeply distressing, is President Obama's embrace of that radical view and rejection of the rule of law. Despite running on promises to return the country to the proper constitutional balance, President Obama's Justice Department has been pulling out all the stops to kill the major lawsuits challenging the surveillance while giving no indication that the surveillance has ceased.

The administration's arguments are not addressing the merits of the legal claims, but instead are seeking to prevent real judicial review of the surveillance programs and thereby avoid the crucial constitutional questions. If our system of checks and balances is to continue and if our nation is to remain faithful to the individual liberties on which it was founded, then the Bush and Obama administrations must defend their surveillance program on the merits before a court of law.

Biometric Databases Make It Impossible for Innocent Citizens to Avoid Scrutiny

Daniel Sayani

Daniel Sayani is a journalist who analyzes and reports on a wide variety of issues.

The FBI announced last week [in mid-March 2011] that its new identification system has reached its initial operating capacity. Known as Next Generation Identification (NGI), the Lockheed Martin–built program serves as an incremental upgrade of the FBI's Integrated Automated Fingerprint Identification System, or IAFIS—which will revolutionize law enforcement's ability to process fingerprints.

NGI provides automated fingerprint and latent search capabilities, electronic image storage and electronic exchange of fingerprints to more than 18,000 law enforcement agencies and other authorized criminal justice partners 24/7. Upon completion, the system will have the ability to process fingerprint transactions much more effectively and accurately.

"The implementation announced today represents a tremendous achievement in enhancing our identification services. Already, we're seeing how the NGI system is revolutionizing fingerprint identification in support of our mission," said Louis E. Grever, executive assistant director of the FBI Science and Technology Branch.

"Lockheed Martin was there supporting the FBI when IAFIS went live in 1999, and we're thrilled to be here for NGI today," affirmed Linda Gooden, executive vice president of Lockheed Martin Information Systems and Global Solutions.

"Technology like this is a powerful tool when it comes to protecting America's citizens, and we're proud to serve as a partner in that mission."

"While IAFIS has been effective, criminal and terrorist threats have evolved over the past decade. Today's environment demands faster and more advanced identification capabilities," said Assistant Director Daniel D. Roberts, of the FBI Criminal Justice Information Services Division. "NGI represents a quantum leap in fingerprint identification that will help us in solving investigations, preventing crime, and apprehending criminals and terrorists."

Lockheed Martin, the nation's largest recipient of defense industry contracts, and a leader in the field of biometrics, says that the new technology enhances the FBI's background-check programs by giving investigators expanded and more timely access to fingerprints. They also note that they see the FBI contract as a means by which biometric surveillance can be increased: a press release from the defense contractor states that "[W]hile this meets the challenges of today, tomorrow holds the possibility of developing iris scanners, genetic scanners, and other advanced biometric solutions."

The biometrics company was awarded the $1 billion contract to develop the new, enhanced identification system in February 2008. According to Leslie Holoweiko, a Lockheed representative, the company has also received government contracts to open the Biometric Experimentation and Advanced Concepts (BEACON™) center in White Hall, W.Va., to serve as a collaborative center in the development of integrated biometrics solutions for both current and future initiatives. She also indicates that the company is the lead systems integrator for the Registered Traveler program led by Verified Identity Pass, Inc. Lockheed is also the lead contractor for the Transportation Worker Identification Credential (TWIC) program, a TSA [Transportation Security Administration] initiative to protect ports by issuing a biometrically-based credential to vetted workers requiring unescorted access to the ports.

World's Largest Biometric Database

To date, the NGI system is the world's largest biometric database, which the FBI expects to make available to a wide variety of federal, state, and local agencies, all in the name of keeping America safe from terrorists (and illegal immigration). The FBI also intends to retain (upon employer request) the fingerprints of any employee who has undergone a criminal background check, and will inform the employer if the employee is ever arrested or charged with a crime.

The increasing use of biometrics for identification ... is drawing criticism from those who worry that people's bodies will become de facto national identification cards.

The *Washington Post* also says that the NGI database relies heavily upon real-time (or very nearly real-time) comparisons. This could include general face recognition, specific feature comparison (notable scars, shape of the earlobe, etc.), walking stride, speech patterns, and iris comparisons. To date, facial-recognition technology hasn't exactly reshaped the face of law enforcement.

The increasing use of biometrics for identification is raising questions about the increasing inability of Americans to avoid unwanted scrutiny. It is drawing criticism from those who worry that people's bodies will become de facto national identification cards. Critics say that such government initiatives should not proceed without proof that the technology really can pick a criminal out of a crowd.

The use of biometric data is increasing throughout the government. For the past two years, the Defense Department has been storing in a database the images of fingerprints, irises, and faces of more than 1.5 million Iraqi and Afghan detainees, Iraqi citizens, and foreigners who need access to U.S. military bases. The Pentagon also collects DNA samples from some Iraqi detainees, which are stored separately.

The Department of Homeland Security [DHS] has been using iris scans at some airports to verify the identity of travelers who have passed background checks and who want to move through lines quickly. The department is also looking to apply iris- and face-recognition techniques to other programs. The DHS already has a database of millions of sets of fingerprints, which includes records collected from U.S. and foreign travelers stopped at borders for criminal violations, from U.S. citizens adopting children overseas, and from visa applicants abroad. Therefore, there could be multiple records of one person's prints.

"It's going to be an essential component of tracking," warned Barry Steinhardt, director of the Technology and Liberty Project of the American Civil Liberties Union. "It's enabling the Always On Surveillance Society."

Advocates of civil liberties (inspired by John Locke's belief that one's natural rights to life, liberty, and property entail a fundamental right to be free from government intrusions into bodily autonomy) also are concerned that the creation of this biometric database can unconstitutionally infringe on the Fourth Amendment rights of the American people. (The *New American* discussed many of these concerns in a previous analysis of the DHS's creation of a genetic scanning program, which could easily metastasize into a government DNA database.)

Biometric Data Is Forever

Privacy advocates also are concerned about the ability of people to correct false information. "Unlike say, a credit card number, biometric data is forever," noted Paul Saffo, a Silicon Valley technology forecaster. He voiced his concern that the FBI, whose computer technology record has been marred by expensive failures, could not guarantee the data's security, "If someone steals and spoofs your iris image, you can't just get a new eyeball," he explained.

A traveler may walk down an airport corridor and allow his face and iris images to be captured without ever stepping up to a kiosk and looking into a camera.

By 2013, the FBI says that it hopes to expand the NGI system to "fuse" fingerprint-, face-, iris-, and palm-matching capabilities into one mega-database, according to Kimberly Del Greco, the FBI's biometric services section chief. In addition, Lawrence Hornak, director of the West Virginia University Center for Identification Technology Research (CITeR), indicated that the government's goal is "ubiquitous use of biometrics." A traveler may walk down an airport corridor and allow his face and iris images to be captured without ever stepping up to a kiosk and looking into a camera, he said.

For those who champion constitutional rights, this latest milestone represents yet another step in the erosion of natural rights and individual liberties, and a turn toward a more robust, authoritarian police state.

Military Satellites Spy on People Within the United States

Barry Steinhardt

Barry Steinhardt recently retired as the director of the Technology and Liberty Program at the American Civil Liberties Union.

Government satellite technology is representative of a larger trend that has been under way in the United States: the seemingly inexorable drift toward a surveillance society.

The explosion of computers, cameras, sensors, wireless communication, GPS, biometrics, and other technologies in just the last 10 years is feeding what can be described as a surveillance monster that is growing silently in our midst. Scarcely a month goes by in which we don't read about some new high-tech method for invading privacy, from face recognition to implantable microchips, data-mining to DNA chips, electronic identity systems, access passes that record our comings and goings, and even plans for RFID [radio-frequency identification] radio computer chips in our clothing and other consumer goods. The fact is, there are no longer any *technical* barriers to the creation of the surveillance society.

While the technological bars are falling away, we should be strengthening the laws and institutions that protect against abuse.

A Surveillance Society?

Unfortunately, even as this surveillance monster grows in power, we are weakening the legal chains that keep it from trampling our privacy. We should be responding to intrusive

Barry Steinhardt, "Testimony: The Privacy and Civil Liberties Implications of Domestic Spy Satellites," House Committee on Homeland Security, September 6, 2007. www.homeland.house.gov.

new technologies by building stronger restraints to protect our privacy; instead, we are doing the opposite—loosening regulations on government surveillance, watching passively as private surveillance grows unchecked, and contemplating the introduction of tremendously powerful new surveillance infrastructures that will tie all this information together.

The government's use of military spy satellites to monitor its own people represents another large step toward a surveillance society.

Given this larger context in which the plans for domestic deployment of our spy satellites are being made, several conclusions are clear:

- This step is part of a trend of turning our nation's surveillance capabilities inward upon our own population.

- If spy satellites are to be deployed domestically, it is vital that the most rigorous checks and balances and oversight mechanisms be put in place.

- There is much that we do not know about our nation's satellite surveillance capabilities.

- A moratorium should be placed on this program until Congress receives answers to the key questions about the program, enacts far-seeing statutory protections against its misuse, and explicitly authorizes the program.

The government's use of military spy satellites to monitor its own people represents another large step toward a surveillance society. Our response—and especially the Congressional response—to this new technology will serve as a test case for how wisely we handle the introduction of a powerful new surveillance technology by the government.

Chairman [Rep. Bennie] Thompson and the Committee have taken an important first step in calling this hearing. But other steps must be taken before this program is allowed to go into effect.

There is much that we do not know about this classified system of spy satellites that was designed for military and foreign intelligence purposes. One fact seems plain:

The satellites have capabilities that far exceed those that are in commercial use.

- They have far better resolution. They can see much more clearly and in greater detail.

- While perhaps not as nimble as they have been portrayed in popular entertainment like *24* or *Enemy of the State*, they apparently do have advanced targeting capabilities.

- They can and do see far more than the human eye. There is much we do not know about their ability to pierce opaque objects, but there is every reason to believe they have some (and perhaps substantial) capacity to do exactly that with the power to convey information about how Americans live and work.

- The military and the intelligence community are at the cutting edge of technological change. The satellites are only going to grow more powerful and capable and change will occur quickly.

The Congress needs to act before our military satellites are deployed domestically. You must act before they are turned on our own people.

It is vital that the most rigorous checks and balances and oversight mechanisms be put in place. The domestic use of spy satellites represents a potential monster in the making, and we need to put some chains on this beast before it grows into something we cannot control.

Current Laws Not Strong Enough

The Department of Defense (DoD) and Department of Homeland Security (DHS) have strongly implied in media reports that there is no legal guidance available to them regarding the use of spy satellites. Nothing could be further from the truth. Congress has thought long and carefully about this issue. Beginning in 1981 and steadily updated over the subsequent two and a half decades, Congress has passed detailed statutory guidance as to how the military is to act when involved with civilian law enforcement. . . .

Military involvement in civilian law enforcement is something that Americans have always regarded with deep unease and the Posse Comitatus Act reflects those concerns. When Congress updated the Posse Comitatus Act it did so with careful deliberation. Authorizations for military involvement were limited, originally only allowing the military to operate directly in one area: suppression of the drug trade at the border. Congress generally limited the military to indirect assistance—loaning equipment and training civilian police. Direct action by the military could only be undertaken outside the United States.

These laws have been updated over the years, but the basic prohibitions have remained intact: direct assistance by the military is permitted only for a limited number of crimes, and monitoring of individuals is largely limited to the area outside the continental United States. DoD and DHS simply cannot be allow to step in and pretend that none of these rules apply and that this substantial body of law does not exist.

While there is substantial law to be applied in this situation, it may not be sufficient to contend with the new reality of military spy technology stationed miles above the earth, rather than soldiers with their boots on the ground. . . .

The might of the military is a dangerous thing in a democracy—a tiger in our midst—and must be carefully bounded and restricted in light of the experience of so many societies throughout history where the military has become a political force with power that comes not from the ballot box but from the barrel of a gun—or the lens of a camera. . . .

The Need for Oversight

Of course, without proper checks and balances there is no guarantee that appropriate limits would be observed. Whenever we contemplate the introduction of tremendously powerful new technologies into our domestic arena, our current generation and the current Congress needs to think like Founding Fathers, and Mothers. It was not clear in 1776 what the threats to freedom and democracy would be as the new nation developed, but the Founders were wise enough to put in place a robust system of checks and balances that has withstood the full range of human folly and perfidy for over 200 years. When it comes to spy satellite technology, we may be living in the equivalent of the year 1789 right now. Put another way, we may be looking at a potential monster that is still in its infancy. And if this technology is going to be permitted to be turned inward upon the American people, we need absolute certainty we have the right kind of restraints in place to ensure that, as it grows and evolves in ways we cannot predict, it will not trample on Americans' privacy or other rights. . . .

Spy satellites may have or gain the capability of producing live, moving images like that from a video camera.

The striking thing about our spy satellites is just how much we do not know about them. And it's difficult to draw conclusions about the domestic use of spy satellites when we don't know what they're capable of. In order to craft the right restraints, we need to know just what this monster looks like— and how it is likely to grow.

For example, we do not even know the answer to perhaps the most basic question: what resolution they are capable of. We know Google can go to half a meter, and experts outside the intelligence community say that government satellites exceed that. But, we do not know by how much.

Government satellite images presumably differ in several ways from publicly available online images provided by Google, Microsoft and other Web providers. Online images are merely snapshots taken at most once every few months. Spy satellites may have or gain the capability of producing live, moving images like that from a video camera. Satellites may also be capable of sweeping through much greater geographical areas, and/or of quickly moving their lenses to examine a particular spot within a much greater area at a moment's notice. And they also have capabilities such as radar and infrared imaging. And of course, they can observe ground activities silently and invisibly.

Is law enforcement being seduced by the siren call ... of really cool toys?

We do not know what they can do in terms of penetrating roofs or other structures, live monitoring, the scanning of large geographical areas, the use of artificial intelligence to guide imaging, or other capabilities that we might not even think of. Without knowing the answers to such questions, we cannot even begin to evaluate their potential threat to our privacy.

There is a lot of discussion and speculation about this topic on the Internet and elsewhere, and many experts have ideas of what the limits of this technology are. Undoubtedly, many will emphasize those limits to you in trying to downplay the privacy threat of this technology.

But Americans have the right not just to be free of secret government spying of their innocent activities, but also to have *confidence* that they are not susceptible to the constant possibility of being invisibly observed. So in our view the government must completely declassify and disclose publicly the full extent of the technological capabilities of any satellites that will be aimed at the American people, and you, Congress, must think like Founding Fathers and institute checks and balances that would be strong enough to protect Americans' privacy even in the face of every gee-whiz satellite capability that Hollywood has ever imagined. . . .

Advantages of Spy Satellites

Are there really serious advantages that spy satellites can provide to police and Homeland Security agencies that cannot be provided by commercial satellite images of the type available on the Internet or elsewhere? If so, what are those uses? Are the advantages provided by this program substantial enough to counterbalance its threat to our privacy? Or is this just another example of an arm of our security establishment seeking to find new missions and new reasons for being in order to expand its budgets and bureaucratic reach? Or is law enforcement being seduced by the siren call (to which many of us are susceptible) of really cool toys?

If this new program does not actually show substantial promise in making people safer, the matter should end there. There is no need to engage in detailed balancing tests or evaluations of a program's effect on privacy if it is not going to increase security. . . .

Satellites are but one of many powerful new technologies that are entering our lives at this exciting point in our history. Many of those new technologies promise wonderful new innovations and conveniences—but many, in the absence of due concern and care over their effect on privacy, and in the absence of strong privacy regulations, threaten to become an out-of-control monster that moves us closer than ever to a genuine surveillance society. Congress needs to craft sufficiently strong restraints on this program to ensure that it does *not* go out of control—to protect Americans against the potential for unacceptable uses of satellite surveillance. And it should treat military spy satellites as a test case for how other technologies should be handled, ideally backed up by an overarching privacy law that will create more clarity and stability of expectations for Americans living in an era of constant change.

Powerful Surveillance Cameras in Public Places Can Invade People's Privacy

Gina Harkins

At the time of writing, Gina Harkins was a graduate student at the Medill School of Journalism at Northwestern University and a fellow in Medill's National Security Reporting Project.

New cameras on the Chicago Transit Authority [CTA] are so powerful that they can tell what you're reading while standing on the platform. The new biometrics surveillance the FBI contracted out might be able to recognize faces, scars, tattoos or perform iris scans. Pattern recognition on surveillance cameras may soon recognize if a fight is occurring or a suspicious suitcase is left at an intersection without the need of human operators reviewing the feed.

So do these methods keep us safe? Or invade our privacy?

From 2006 through 2010, the CTA received grants from the Department of Homeland Security totaling $22.6 million to install cameras at rail stations and rail yards. Lockheed Martin, a global security company, won a $1 billion contract to create biometrics surveillance and databases.

As we approach the 10th anniversary of 9/11, are we safer because of these advancements? Or do we more readily give up some civil liberties in the process? Have we kept our balance between the two?

Ed Yohnka, director of communication and public policy at ACLU Illinois said he's still waiting for the balance.

"I have been hearing for almost 10 years now that we needed to balance liberty and security," Yohnka said. "But I have to say, I'm still waiting for the balance. Every single thing—warrantless wiretapping, facial recognition, the plethora of security cameras and Big Brother—would not have been accepted before."

The debate between surveillance and crime prevention has existed for decades.

While there might be some benefits . . . the public should be aware [of] how invasive the new technology is.

Steve Chapman's recent column [from early May 2011] about this issue in the *Chicago Tribune* questioned the effectiveness of cameras. Chapman wrote:

> Nancy La Vigne, director of the Justice Policy Center at the Urban Institute in Washington, has directed a study of the impact of cameras in Chicago, Baltimore and Washington, D.C. Her preliminary findings, due to be finalized and published this year, are that they can indeed curb crime—and at a bargain price.

But with funding from the Department of Homeland Security for such projects, Yohnka said more research needs to be done on the effectiveness of public surveillance.

"The Department of Homeland Security has kind of been the Daddy Warbucks of these types of surveillance projects throughout the last few years," Yohnka said. And while there might be some benefits, he said the public should be aware [of] how invasive the new technology is.

Invasion of Privacy

"I think the most important thing to know is just how invasive and intrusive they are," Yohnka said of new high-powered cameras. "They are more powerful than any other surveillance system we have seen in other places. The ability to magnify many times over what the human eye can see is a very powerful tool."

Brad Hunter, 30, of Northbrook, takes the El [Chicago's elevated train system] a couple times a month into the city from the suburbs. "I feel these cameras are beneficial because they create a better sense of safety and security," Hunter said. "But while higher resolution cameras aid in detective work, I am not sure I would want the FBI investigating me based on what I was reading on the train either."

The number of cameras might also allow for the government to locate people as they travel to places they might like to keep private, Yohnka said. This could include political rallies, psychiatrist appointments or a business deal, he said.

Yohnka also worries that Americans are becoming more accepting of surveillance in a post-9/11 world.

"Technology makes it easier to keep these huge databases. As more and more information is gathered, Americans become desensitized to these types of measures."

The National Strategy for Information Sharing Protects Americans' Privacy Rights

Executive Office of the President of the United States

The Executive Office of the President of the United States comprises the immediate staff of the US president and is headed by the White House chief of staff.

Those responsible for combating terrorism must have access to timely and accurate information regarding those who want to attack us, their plans and activities, and the targets that they intend to attack. That information guides our efforts to:

- identify rapidly both immediate and long-term threats;

- identify persons involved in terrorism-related activities; and

- implement information-driven and risk-based detection, prevention, deterrence, response, protection, and emergency management efforts.

Experience has shown that there is no single source for information related to terrorism. It is derived by gathering, fusing, analyzing, and evaluating relevant information from a broad array of sources on a continual basis. Important information can come through the efforts of the Intelligence Community, Federal, State, tribal, and local law enforcement and homeland security authorities, other government agencies (e.g., the Department of Transportation, the Department of Health and Human Services), and the private sector (e.g., the transportation, healthcare, financial, and information technol-

National Strategy for Information Sharing: Successes and Challenges in Improving Terrorism-Related Information Sharing, Washington, DC: The White House, 2007. Courtesy of The White House.

ogy sectors). Commonly referred to as homeland security information, terrorism information, or law enforcement information, this wide-ranging information can be found across all levels of government as well as in the private sector.

Guiding Principles

This *Strategy* provides the vision for how our Nation will best use and build upon the information sharing innovations which have emerged post-September 11 in order to develop a fully coordinated and integrated information sharing capability that supports our efforts to combat terrorism. The *Strategy* is founded on the following core principles and understandings:

- Effective information sharing comes through strong partnerships among Federal, State, local, and tribal authorities, private sector organizations, and our foreign partners and allies.

- Information acquired for one purpose, or under one set of authorities, might provide unique insights when combined, in accordance with applicable law, with seemingly unrelated information from other sources, and therefore we must foster a culture of awareness in which people at all levels of government remain cognizant of the functions and needs of others and use knowledge and information from all sources to support counterterrorism efforts.

- Information sharing must be woven into all aspects of counterterrorism activity, including preventive and protective actions, actionable responses, criminal and counterterrorism investigative activities, event preparedness, and response to and recovery from catastrophic events.

- The procedures, processes, and systems that support information sharing must draw upon and integrate existing technical capabilities and must respect established authorities and responsibilities.

- State and major urban area fusion centers represent a valuable information sharing resource and should be incorporated into the national information sharing framework, which will require that fusion centers achieve a baseline level of capability to gather, process, share, and utilize information and operate in a manner that respects individuals' privacy rights and other legal rights protected by U.S. laws. . . .

With proper planning we can have both enhanced privacy protections and increased information sharing.

Protecting the rights of Americans is a core facet of our information sharing efforts. While we must zealously protect our Nation from the real and continuing threat of terrorist attacks, we must just as zealously protect the information privacy rights and other legal rights of Americans. With proper planning we can have both enhanced privacy protections and increased information sharing—and in fact, we must achieve this balance at all levels of government, in order to maintain the trust of the American people. The President reaffirmed this in his December 16, 2005, Memorandum to the Heads of Executive Departments and Agencies.

At the direction of the President, the Attorney General and the Director of National Intelligence developed a set of Privacy Guidelines to ensure the information privacy and other legal rights of Americans are protected in the development and use of the ISE [information sharing environment]. The Privacy Guidelines provide a consistent framework for identifying information that is subject to privacy protection, assessing applicable privacy rules, implementing appropriate protections, and ensuring compliance. An array of laws, directives, and policies provide substantive privacy protections for personally identifiable information. The parameters of those protections vary depending on the rules that apply to particular agencies and the information they are proposing to share. As described below, however, the Guidelines demand more than mere compliance with the laws; they require executive departments and agencies to take pro-active and explicit actions to ensure the balance between information privacy and security is maintained, as called for by the *National Commission on Terrorist Attacks Upon the United States*. The full text of the ISE Privacy Guidelines can be found at www.ise.gov.

Core Privacy Principles

The Privacy Guidelines build on a set of core principles that Federal departments and agencies must follow. Those principles require specific, uniform action and reflect basic privacy protections and best practices. Agencies must:

- share protected information only to the extent it is terrorism information, homeland security information, or law enforcement information related to terrorism;

- identify and review the protected information to be shared within the ISE;

- enable ISE participants to determine the nature of the protected information to be shared and its legal restrictions (e.g., "this record contains individually identifiable information about a U.S. citizen");

- assess, document, and comply with all applicable laws and policies;

- establish data accuracy, quality, and retention procedures;

- deploy adequate security measures to safeguard protected information;

- implement adequate accountability, enforcement, and audit mechanisms to verify compliance;

- establish a redress process consistent with legal authorities and mission requirements;

- implement the guidelines through appropriate changes to business processes and systems, training, and technology;

- make the public aware of the agency's policies and procedures as appropriate;

- ensure agencies disclose protected information to non-Federal entities—including State, local, tribal, and foreign governments—only if the non-Federal entities provide comparable protections; and

- state, local, and tribal governments are required to designate a senior official accountable for implementation.

Successful implementation of the Privacy Guidelines requires a governance structure to monitor compliance and to revise the Guidelines as we gain more experience. The President, therefore, directed the Program Manager to establish the ISE Privacy Guidelines Committee. The Committee is chaired by representatives of the Attorney General and the Director of National Intelligence, and consists of the Privacy Officials of the departments and agencies of the Information Sharing Council. The Committee seeks to ensure consistency and standardization, as well as serve as a forum to share best practices and resolve agency concerns.

Law Enforcement Agencies Need the Ability to Intercept All Telecommunications

Mark A. Marshall

Mark A. Marshall is chief of police in Smithfield, Virginia, and president of the International Association of Chiefs of Police.

In the United States, there are more than 18,000 law enforcement agencies and well over 800,000 officers who patrol our state highways and the streets of our communities each and every day. A great number of those officers also use electronic surveillance as they investigate crimes. Each day, state, local, tribal and federal law enforcement agencies use lawful electronic surveillance as a critical tool for enforcing the nation's laws and protecting the citizens they serve. Moreover, electronic evidence is now a routine issue in all crimes and at most crime scenes.

The IACP [International Association of Chiefs of Police] believes that lawful interception of voice and data communications is one of the most valuable investigative tools available to law enforcement in identifying and crippling criminal and terrorist organizations. Understandably, there is an increased volume and complexity of today's communication services and technologies. And, the evolution and development of communication devices has had a significant impact on law enforcement's ability to conduct electronic surveillance, as well as to recover valuable evidence from communication devices. Additionally, legal authorities and mandates have not kept pace with changing technology. CALEA, or the Communications Assistance for Law Enforcement Act, for example, does not cover many types of services that are routinely used by criminals.

The advanced features of today's phones can process more information about where people have been, who they know and are calling, what they are texting, pictures they have and are sending, as well as larger amounts of data than ever before. Information recovered can also produce connections to other media like Facebook and Twitter, contact lists, call history, calendars, GPS waypoints and email. If properly recovered, this sort of stored data on communication devices has great investigative and intelligence value to assist law enforcement with investigations.

Many agencies that need to be able to conduct electronic surveillance of real time communications are on the verge of "Going Dark" because they are increasingly unable to access, intercept, collect and process wire or electronic communications information when they are lawfully authorized to do so. This serious intercept capability gap often undercuts state, local, and tribal law enforcement agencies' efforts to investigate criminal activity such as organized crime, drug-related offenses, child abduction, child exploitation, prison escape, and other threats to public safety.

Laws Must Be Updated

This must change—law enforcement must be able to effectively use lawful electronic surveillance to combat terrorism and fight crime. Law enforcement needs the federal government to generate a uniform set of standards and guidelines to assist in this exploration. In order for law enforcement to maintain its ability to conduct electronic surveillance, laws must be updated to require companies that provide individuals with the ability to communicate to also provide law enforcement with the ability to lawfully intercept those communications in a timely and cost effective manner.

In September of 2010, the Law Enforcement Executive Forum (LEEF), comprised of law enforcement executives, including many from the IACP, released a plan to address the spectrum of issues related to electronic surveillance and to law enforcement's ability to recover and process data stored on communication devices. This plan, National Domestic Communications Assistance Center (NDCAC) Proposal, calls for a strategy to be created to address issues related to maintaining law enforcement's ability to conduct court authorized electronic surveillance. For instance, to determine if a solution within the law enforcement community exists and promote knowledge-sharing among law enforcement agencies and groups regarding technical, legal, policy, and other issues.

Many agencies that need to be able to conduct electronic surveillance of real time communications are . . . increasingly unable to access, intercept, collect and process wire or electronic communications information when they are lawfully authorized to do so.

The Proposal also calls on Congress and the Administration to make funding available to establish the National Domestic Communications Assistance Center. The Center would leverage the research and development efforts of the law enforcement community with respect to lawful electronic surveillance capabilities and the ability to obtain communications device information. The Center would also facilitate the sharing of technology between law enforcement agencies. Finally, the Center would partner with industry to develop CALEA-related technical standards for services beyond those already being addressed by the FBI. The IACP fully supports The Proposal.

The IACP believes that carriers must be required to install, deploy and make available to law enforcement a solution to assist with lawfully authorized electronic surveillance of telecommunication services prior to or concurrent with the release of communications products to the public. The IACP also strongly urges that telecommunications carriers provide law enforcement agencies service for cost and not retail value.

The IACP calls on Congress to take into account the National Domestic Communications Assistance Center (NDCAC) Proposal and use the Proposal's recommendations to create a national strategy to assist state, local and tribal law enforcement in addressing the technical developments and issues related to electronic surveillance.

State, local, tribal and federal law enforcement are doing all that we can to protect our communities from increasing crime rates and the specter of terrorism—both in our streets and in the many communications devices available today, but we cannot do it alone. We need the full support and assistance of the federal government and clear guidance and regulations on our use of lawful interception of voice and data communications to aid us in successfully investigating and prosecuting the most dangerous of criminals.

The PATRIOT Act Does Not Violate Americans' Right to Privacy

Nathan A. Sales

Nathan A. Sales is a law professor at George Mason University School of Law and a former deputy assistant secretary in the Office of Policy at the US Department of Homeland Security.

The USA PATRIOT Act is a vital set of tools in our ongoing struggle against al Qaeda and like-minded terrorists. This is especially true of the three authorities that are up for renewal this year: "roving wiretaps," "business records," and "lone wolf." Notwithstanding the PATRIOT Act's controversial reputation, these three provisions are actually quite modest. In many cases, they simply let counterterrorism agents use some of the same techniques that ordinary criminal investigators have been using for decades—techniques that the federal courts repeatedly have upheld. Plus, each of these authorities contains elaborate safeguards—including prior judicial review—to help prevent abuses from taking place. Indeed, some of the PATRIOT Act's protections are even *stronger* than the ones from the world of ordinary law enforcement.

Roving Wiretaps

The policy rationale for "roving wiretaps"—in essence, court orders that apply to particular *people*, rather than particular *devices*—is fairly straightforward. Sophisticated targets like drug kingpins, mob bosses, spies, and terrorists are trained to thwart electronic surveillance by constantly switching communications devices or methods. They might use "burner" cell phones, for instance, or they might repeatedly swap out their phones' SIM [subscriber identity module] cards. The result is a drawn-out game of cat and mouse. Investigators obtain a court order to tap a suspect's new phone only to discover that he has already switched to an even newer one. So it's back to the judge for a fresh warrant. Not only is this cycle a waste of investigators' scarce time and resources, it also runs the risk that agents will miss critical communications in the gap before the court can issue an updated order.

Congress largely solved this problem for criminal investigators two and a half decades ago when it enacted the Electronic Communications Privacy Act of 1986. . . .

Of course, terrorists and spies can be just as adept at evading surveillance as drug dealers and mobsters. Maybe even more so. And so the PATRIOT Act allows national security investigators to use the same sort of technique as their law enforcement counterparts. Section 206 of the law permits roving wiretaps under the Foreign Intelligence Surveillance Act of 1978 (FISA) where "the actions of the target of the application may have the effect of thwarting the identification of a specified person." The basic idea here is to level the playing field between criminal cases and terrorism cases. If a roving wiretap is good enough for [fictional mobster] Tony Soprano, Congress concluded, it's good enough for [9/11 terrorist] Mohamed Atta.

Significantly, the PATRIOT Act's roving wiretaps authority contains exacting safeguards to protect privacy and civil liberties. As in the criminal context, a prior court order is necessary. FBI agents can't unilaterally decide to eavesdrop on every phone a person uses. They have to appear before the Foreign Intelligence Surveillance Court and convince a federal judge that there is probable cause to believe that the target is a "foreign power" (such as a foreign country or a foreign terrorist organization) or an "agent of a foreign power" (such as a spy or a terrorist). . . .

Federal courts agree that Title III's roving wiretaps authority is constitutional, and that consensus provides strong support for the constitutionality of roving wiretaps under the PATRIOT Act.... In short, there is a broad judicial consensus that, as the Ninth Circuit put it in another case, "[r]oving wiretaps are an appropriate tool to investigate individuals ... who use cloned cellular phone numbers and change numbers frequently to avoid detection."

Investigators must follow a rigorous set of procedures that "minimize the acquisition and retention, and prohibit the dissemination," of Americans' private data.

Finally, let me say a few words about "John Doe" roving wiretaps—surveillance in which the FISA court order describes the target but does not indicate his precise name or the precise facilities to be tapped. The risk of misuse under the PATRIOT Act seems to me fairly low. There may be times when investigators don't yet know the specific identity of the terrorist in question. (Indeed, the need to learn more about the target is precisely why one conducts surveillance in the first place.) In these circumstances, investigators need not indicate his name, but they still must provide the FISA court with a "description of the specific target," which might include the names of his terrorist associates, his age, his country of origin, or other biographical details. Second, investigators still must comply with the bedrock requirement that they establish, to the satisfaction of the FISA court, probable cause to believe that the person to be surveilled is a foreign power or an agent of a foreign power. ...

Third, any risk of overcollection—i.e., the possibility that investigators might inadvertently intercept communications involving innocent third parties—is mitigated by FISA's minimization requirement: Investigators must follow a rigorous set of procedures that "minimize the acquisition and retention, and prohibit the dissemination," of Americans' private data. Fourth, the active involvement of the FISA court stands as a significant bulwark against any misuse. Not only does the court provide oversight before any surveillance is approved, in the form of ex ante [beforehand] judicial review. It also provides ongoing oversight while the surveillance is taking place: Investigators who operate a roving wiretap must alert the FISA court no more than ten days after they begin monitoring any new facility, and they must explain the "facts and circumstances" that justify their "belief that each new facility or place at which the electronic surveillance is directed is or was being used, or is about to be used, by the target." The combination of these safeguards should adequately ensure that roving wiretaps do not infringe upon important privacy interests.

Business Records

Section 215 of the PATRIOT Act—the so-called "business records" provision—authorizes the national security equivalent of grand jury subpoenas. Criminals often leave behind trails of evidence in their everyday interactions with banks, credit card companies and other businesses. Federal grand juries routinely issue subpoenas to these entities in investigations that range from narcotics crimes to health care fraud. When a subpoena is issued, the recipient is required to turn over "any books, papers, documents, data, or other objects the subpoena designates." The recipient must do so whenever there is a "reasonable possibility that the category of materials the Government seeks will produce information relevant to the general subject of the grand jury's investigation."

The PATRIOT Act amended FISA to establish a comparable mechanism for national security investigators to obtain the same sorts of materials. . . .

In fact, there are several respects in which section 215's safeguards are even stricter than those that apply in the grand jury context. . . .

The constitutional principles concerning government access to third party records have been settled for decades, and these precedents strongly support the PATRIOT Act's business records authority. A long line of Supreme Court case law confirms that there is no "reasonable expectation of privacy" in the information a person conveys to businesses and other third parties. As a result, the government's efforts to acquire such data—as with grand jury subpoenas, for example—do not amount to "searches" within the meaning of the Fourth Amendment. Investigators therefore need not secure a warrant or demonstrate probable cause. . . . If mere relevance is all that's required to obtain business records in ordinary criminal investigations, it is not readily apparent why something more than that should be required to obtain the same materials in national security investigations.

Solitary actors . . . are capable of causing just as much death and destruction as those who are formally members of [terrorist] networks.

Section 215 isn't just known as the "business records" provision, of course. It's also known, unflatteringly, as the "libraries" provision. Section 215 isn't aimed at libraries, and the Justice Department has indicated to Congress that the provision has never been used to obtain library or bookstore records. While section 215 conceivably might be applied to libraries or bookstores, it isn't unique in that respect: It's not unusual for grand juries to demand library records in regular criminal cases. For instance, during the Unabomber investigation, grand juries issued subpoenas to a half dozen university libraries; investigators wanted to know who had checked out various works that were cited in the "Unabomber Manifesto." . . .

Lone Wolf

The third provision that is up for renewal this year is known as the "lone wolf" fix. (Note that lone wolf wasn't part of the

PATRIOT Act. Congress adopted it in the Intelligence Reform and Terrorism Prevention Act of 2004 (IRTPA), and also subjected it to PATRIOT's sunset provision.) As a result of this measure, counterterrorism investigators may obtain the FISA court's approval to conduct electronic surveillance of certain international terrorists even if there is not yet enough evidence to formally link them to a foreign terrorist organization.

Two distinct yet related policy considerations suggest a need for lone wolf surveillance. First, there's the evidentiary problem. It may be difficult for investigators to establish that a given suspect is a member of, or otherwise has ties to, a foreign terrorist organization. The problem is likely to be especially acute during the early stages of an investigation, when agents are just beginning to assemble a picture of the target's intentions. According to the 9/11 Commission, the FBI faced this predicament in the weeks before 9/11. Agents believed that Zacarias Moussaoui—then in federal custody on immigration charges—was a terrorist. Investigators hadn't yet connected Moussaoui to any foreign terrorists, so it was unclear whether they could use FISA to search his apartment or laptop. The 9/11 Commission later speculated that, if agents had investigated Moussaoui more fully, they might have unraveled the entire September 11 plot.

Second, there's the growing danger of entrepreneurial terrorism. . . . Solitary actors who are inspired by foreign terrorist organizations like al Qaeda, or radical clerics like Anwar al-Awlaki, are capable of causing just as much death and destruction as those who are formally members of such networks. Indeed, some of the most chilling terrorist plots to emerge in recent years have involved operatives who may have been acting on their own, not at the direction of an overseas group. . . . This trend toward entrepreneurial terrorism is on the rise and shows no signs of abating. . . .

The lone wolf fix helps investigators overcome these evidentiary difficulties, and meet this evolving terrorist threat, through a simple change to the Foreign Intelligence Surveillance Act. In particular, FISA provides that agents may not conduct surveillance unless they persuade the FISA court that there is probable cause to believe that the target is a "foreign power" or an "agent of a foreign power." Lone wolf tweaked the latter definition. The term "agent of a foreign power" has always included a non-American who is a "member" of "a group engaged in international terrorism or activities in preparation therefor." Now, the term also includes a non-American who "engages in international terrorism or activities in preparation therefor." . . . Note that this authority has a critical restriction: It does not apply to United States persons—i.e., persons who are either U.S. citizens or lawful permanent resident aliens. Americans cannot be surveilled under the lone wolf provision as it currently stands.

This is no time to dismantle the USA PATRIOT Act.

As with the other two authorities that are up for reauthorization, lone wolf features important protections for privacy and civil liberties. Chief among them is the requirement of ex ante [prior] judicial approval. FBI agents cannot start monitoring a suspected lone wolf on their own; they must appear before the FISA court and convince it to authorize the surveillance. Second, lone wolf still requires investigators to establish that a given target has a foreign nexus. The tool can only be used to investigate people who are engaging in "*international* terrorism." . . . Lone wolf thus cannot be used to investigate persons suspected of engaging in domestic terrorism. Finally, FISA's minimization requirement applies to lone wolf surveillance, offering protection to the innocent Americans with whom the lone wolves come into contact.

The terrorist threat isn't going away anytime soon. Al Qaeda and its followers are still mortal dangers to Americans at home and abroad, and Congress should make sure that our counterterrorism agents have the tools they need to detect and disrupt our enemies' bloody plots. This is no time to dismantle the USA PATRIOT Act. The three provisions that are on the verge of expiring—roving wiretaps, business records, and lone wolf—have been on the statute books for years without compromising vital privacy interests or civil liberties. Not only does the PATRIOT Act let counterterrorism agents use some of the same investigative techniques that regular cops and prosecutors have had in their arsenal for years. The act's safeguards and protections are at least as robust as—and in some cases are even more robust than—their law enforcement counterparts. Congress should promptly reauthorize these authorities before they sunset later this year.

Al Qaeda hasn't given up. We can't afford to either.

CHAPTER 3

How Is Technology Affecting Intelligence Gathering?

Overview: Technology Is Transforming the Intelligence Field

John E. McLaughlin

John E. McLaughlin, a former deputy director of the Central Intelligence Agency (CIA), is distinguished practitioner in residence at the Paul H. Nitze School of Advanced International Studies (SAIS) at the Johns Hopkins University.

Retired General Brent Scowcroft, National Security Adviser to former US President George H.W. Bush, once remarked that the "role of intelligence is to narrow the range of uncertainty when difficult national security decisions have to be made." By that standard, the job of intelligence is getting dramatically more difficult as international uncertainties multiply.

One of the underlying forces contributing to this state of affairs is a 'revolution' in science and technology. Technological advances throughout history have continually altered the landscape for this ancient craft. Something as basic as the invention of the wheel or gunpowder had an immediate impact on conflict and power projection, and therefore altered the focus of espionage.

But until the invention of the telegraph in the mid-19th century, the basic techniques of intelligence collection remained essentially unchanged from their description in the sixth century BC by Sun Tzu. Sun Tzu's writings still provide the core precepts for the oldest part of the profession—the recruitment and handling of human spies.

Once adversaries were able to move information rapidly and invisibly through scientific means like the telegraph, the telephone and radios, intelligence officers were faced with new, scientifically-based challenges. These challenges grew exponentially during the 20th century, with unprecedented advances in physics, engineering, communications and photography.

In the 21st century, intelligence will be aided and challenged as never before by technological and scientific advances—advances distinguished by their accelerating pace, the growing synergy among disciplines, and the shrinking time between scientific discoveries and their application.

These trends are evident in fields like information technology, biology and nanotechnology. Computing power is doubling every 18 months, and the world has gone from about 5,000 computers worldwide in the 1950s to an Internet ('wired') population today of more than 1 billion people with access to more than 300 billion webpages. In biology, something that might have earned a doctorate 10 years ago is now the work of technicians.

In the 21st century, intelligence will be aided and challenged as never before by technological and scientific advances.

Undergirding much of the progress in these and other fields is the revolution in nanotechnology, where miniaturization has yet to reach the limits posed by the laws of physics. A metaphor for all of this is the miniaturization of electronic circuitry: a microchip that contained only 29,000 transistors in the 1980s now houses more than a billion—thereby powering many of today's technological 'miracles,' from communications to precision weaponry.

Challenges to Intelligence Officers

The enhancements that these changes bring to intelligence capabilities are offset by myriad challenges. The most basic challenge is one of *innovation*, because the intelligence discipline must always strive to be a lap ahead, technologically—something much harder in an era when more and more sophisticated technology is commercially available, and when adversaries have easy access to it.

An important corollary is that today's technology gives adversaries the potential to *acquire new weapons* more easily and rapidly. The advances in biology, for example, mean that the traditional barriers to non-state creation of biological weapons—strain availability, weaponization technology, and means of delivery—have fallen away.

Along with communications advances come *problems of volume*. Today's intelligence officers run the risk of missing clues as they struggle to mine important nuggets buried in thousands of messages daily. If they are lucky enough to capture, say, a terrorist's electronic media, they will probably have the digital equivalent of a small public library, and will need sophisticated algorithms to isolate the key data.

A related challenge calls for *greater precision* in many parts of the discipline, especially those operating in direct support of the military. Case in point: today's B-2 bomber can simultaneously deliver 16 2,000-pound bombs with pinpoint accuracy on 16 different targets in one pass—making it mandatory that supporting intelligence be accurate to a degree of precision not imagined before in history.

In the end, intelligence is often about assessing and affecting *power relationships in the world*, so practitioners of the craft must be aware of how technology is redefining these relationships. When historians look back 100 years hence, some may call this the 'age of asymmetry,' because the central impact of modern technology has been to erode conventional means of exerting influence, putting greater power for good and evil—the power to persuade, to create and destroy—into the hands of smaller numbers of people. This may be the single most important thing for intelligence officers to keep in mind as they strive to 'narrow the range of uncertainty' in an increasingly uncertain world.

A Great Deal of Valuable Intelligence Is Obtained from Open Sources

Central Intelligence Agency

The Central Intelligence Agency (CIA) is the US government agency responsible for providing national security intelligence assessment to the nation's senior policy makers.

Information does not have to be secret to be valuable. Whether in the blogs we browse, the broadcasts we watch, or the specialized journals we read, there is an endless supply of information that contributes to our understanding of the world. The Intelligence Community generally refers to this information as Open Source Intelligence (OSINT). OSINT plays an essential role in giving the national security community as a whole insight and context at a relatively low cost.

OSINT is drawn from publicly available material, including:

- The Internet

- Traditional mass media (e.g. television, radio, newspapers, magazines)

- Specialized journals, conference proceedings, and think tank studies

- Photos

- Geospatial information (e.g. maps and commercial imagery products)

CIA is responsible for collecting, producing, and promoting open source intelligence through its management of the DNI [director of national intelligence] Open Source Center

"INTelligence: Open Source Intelligence," CIA.gov, July 23, 2010. www.cia.gov.

(OSC). OSC was established on November 1, 2005 in response to recommendations by the Robb-Silberman Commission, and is charged with a unique, Community-wide responsibility.

OSC and its worldwide network of partners have the skills, tools, and access necessary to produce high-quality open source intelligence. These capabilities include translations in over 80 languages; source, trends, and media analyses; specialized video and geospatial services; and rare cultural and subject matter expertise.

To OSC Director Douglas Naquin strong partnerships are absolutely essential.

"Given the variety and scope of the questions we can address through publicly available information, I believe it is incumbent on us to work across organizations—inside and outside government—to make the most effective use of available expertise and capability. We in OSC focus on comparative advantage: If we find an organization or company that can do something particularly well—for example, translations—we will leverage that advantage to the extent we can, allowing us then to focus our resources on what we do best."

Answering New Questions

OSINT has always been an important part of all-source analysis, but continuing advances in information technology have given a voice to even larger numbers of people and made it possible to address new intelligence questions.

"For example, open sources can tell us how various groups overseas react to a speech by the president," Naquin said. "We don't have to settle for the 'official' view but can assess various groups' perceptions as well as track trends over time."

"Just because open source is 'free' or publicly available doesn't mean it is easy," Naquin added. To filter, understand, and analyze the enormous amount of material that comes into OSC 24/7, Open Source Officers (OSO) must be fluent in foreign languages, sensitive to cultural nuances, experts in their field, whether video, geospatial tools, media analysis or library science.

"If a government changes its stance toward the United States, an analyst with a thorough understanding of the language and familiarity with the culture might not only be able to forecast this change but can tell us why," Naquin said. "The ability to combine foreign language skill, cultural knowledge, and advanced search techniques is not common."

An experienced [open source officer] is attuned to changes in tone, word choice, and syntax in official messages from foreign governments and organizations.

Policymakers and other government officials also rely on that expertise to gain a good picture of countries they plan to visit.

"They want to know the environment and various players before they visit," Naquin said. "Not just guidebook information, but details that will help make their visits fruitful. It's surprising what one can find in open sources if one knows where to look."

OSC makes most of the information it collects and processes available both to the Intelligence Community and to the entire U.S. Government. Beyond making this "raw" data available to their all-source counterparts, OSC analysts identify and flag for others new insights or trends from open sources.

An experienced OSO is attuned to changes in tone, word choice, and syntax in official messages from foreign governments and organizations. Comparisons with past statements can provide insights into how the foreign actors view an incident or issue. The analysis can also help identify their "hot buttons" or "red lines."

Challenges and Opportunities

As with all intelligence disciplines, OSINT has its challenges. The sheer volume is daunting, and separating wheat from chaff requires skill, knowledge, and a reliance on sophisticated information technology. It also takes a concerted effort to coordinate with partners to avoid duplication and make the best use of resources, but the payoff in both effectiveness and efficiency is high.

"As I look back over the past couple of years, we've made more significant contributions than even I would have anticipated," Naquin said. "We work, however, at the convergence of the two most dynamic industries: media and information technology. It's like being in a kayak going downstream at the fork of two rivers; the ride will be challenging, but if you have the skill, it's also going to be good."

The Internet, of course, has revolutionized the open source environment. Naquin expects that trend to continue.

"An organization that invests in open source today is akin to an individual who invested in Google in its first year. OSINT has always been an integral component in intelligence, but in five years, I believe the value proposition can only increase. An organization with an appreciation for OSINT's value and potential will be the most effective in the future."

Satellites Play a Vital Role in America's Intelligence-Gathering System

Karoun Demirjian

Karoun Demirjian is a reporter for the Las Vegas Sun.

Whether it was used to take aerial pictures of the area, map the compound, attempt to identify the terrorist mastermind himself, or transmit real-time images of the raid to President Barack Obama, satellite technology played a vital role in the months-long operation in which a band of Navy SEALs killed America's public enemy No. 1, Osama bin Laden.

Responsibility to make sure such satellites are working falls to [Nevada] Rep. Joe Heck and a handful of others in Congress.

When House Speaker John Boehner selected Heck as the only freshman to serve on the small and secretive Select Committee on Intelligence, Heck's assignment was the subcommittee for Technical and Tactical Intelligence, which monitors the government's satellite capacity.

His job seems straightforward: bone up on the network of military, intelligence and commercial satellites, figure out how to improve government-private sector cooperation, and figure out how to update the fleet but also cut costs.

"There are a lot of old satellites," Heck told the *Las Vegas Sun* in late April [2011] a few days after returning from a trip to California to tour several satellite production and launch facilities, and interview engineers about designs and demands of production. He called the trip his "400-level" course in his accelerated education on satellites. "Many were launched with

Karoun Demirjian, "Joe Heck's National Security Role Finds New Urgency after Osama Bin Laden's Death," *Las Vegas Sun*, May 10, 2011. Copyright © 2011 by *Las Vegas Sun*. All rights reserved. Reproduced by permission.

a five-to-10-year life span, but we have satellites up there working that are over 20 years old," he said. "They're working, but on life support."

But Heck's job got a new level of urgency in the aftermath of bin Laden's death.

The system of satellites employed by the U.S. is relatively small, but complex.

The official words on the satellite industry in the days since the successful raid have mostly been ones of praise.

"The outer features of the compound were studied intensively and there were certain assessments made about where individuals were living and where bin Laden and his family were," John Brennan, Obama's counterterrorism chief, told reporters after the raid, referring to satellite images that intelligence operatives had collected. "We were able to monitor in a real-time basis the progress of the operation from its commencement, to its time on target, to the extraction of the remains, and to then the egress off of the target."

The system of satellites employed by the U.S. is relatively small, but complex: The government relies on specialized equipment used for military and intelligence-gathering purposes, and commercial satellites, such as those that enable global positioning systems.

"It's a combination: everything from commercial satellites, to intelligence satellites, to military satellites," Heck said.

There are only about 100 official military satellites circling the globe. That may seem small, but it's actually more than half of all the military satellites in operation worldwide. It's also more satellites than the next-biggest operator, Russia, has in its entire national fleet: military, commercial, or otherwise. China has announced plans to out-orbit the U.S. in the next 10 years, but hasn't yet hit close to its mark.

Public-Private Satellite Networks

Although the satellites used for surveillance activities, such as mapping bin Laden's compound, get the most attention, they're not the largest, or even the most important. That distinction goes to communications, where Heck's spent the most time, recently investigating.

The long-standing dual nature of the satellite industry as public-private partnership . . . creates a complicated pattern of authority.

More than 80 percent of government and military communications takes place across commercial satellite networks that also serve civilians and are managed by private corporations, a balance that leaves even the most top-secret operations susceptible to failures in cybersecurity.

The interconnectedness of the systems means that anything from the transmission of an email, to the flight plan of a drone, could pose potential for a security leak.

The long-standing dual nature of the satellite industry as public-private partnership also creates a complicated pattern of authority. As with most space and defense projects, government contractors are designing and building the satellites. And although military satellites are launched almost exclusively from Cape Canaveral in Florida or Vandenberg Air Force Base in California, it's usually contractors that are doing the launching.

"It's more cost effective to use a commercial provider than a government provider to launch satellites," Heck said.

On his visit to California last month, Heck said he met several contractors, including Northrop Grumman, Boeing, and SpaceX—a company that only does commercial launches—to explore possibilities for future cooperation.

Although Heck expects private contractors will save the government on satellite operation, some experts warn he should think again.

"Ninety percent of what's going on in the military/space field is done by private contractors, because they are the ones who know how to do it," said John Pike, an expert on defense and intelligence policy related to space and director of Global security.org. Because the government has no recourse to private contractors—save new ones who might potentially bid the price of a satellite down—costs are likely to stay where they are, he said.

"Everybody's having too much fun spending all this money," he said.

Satellites aren't the government's best reconnaissance tool—that distinction would go to drones, such as those operated out of Nevada's Creech Air Force Base, which can capture 24/7, full-motion video in real time, instead of still pictures once every two hours—there's also no real alternative to them as an intelligence-gathering tool.

"For most things, you don't need full-motion video; for most things, you just want to know where the airfield is, how many jets do they have on it," Pike said. "Our spy satellites are always the first American government resource on the scene, in any incident, accident, or attack, anywhere on the planet . . . and you never have to worry about airspace."

Starting in a few weeks [in summer 2011] it's going to be Heck's responsibility—behind closed doors—to figure out if there's a leaner way to keep the satellite fleet in fighting shape up in the air.

"It's so critical to our national security, we have to move forward," Heck said. "But we've got to do it in a cost-effective manner."

Unmanned Aerial Vehicles Provide Intelligence During Military Operations

Nate Hale

Nate Hale is the pseudonym of a retired member of the US intelligence community who served for twenty years in military intelligence as an analyst, operations planner, flight commander, briefer, nuclear targeteer, and aircrew member. He now maintains a widely read blog, Formerspook.

There's little doubt that unmanned aerial vehicles [UAVs] have revolutionized modern warfare. Beginning with Israel's Bekka Valley campaign in 1982, and (more recently) with U.S. Predator and Reaper drones in Iraq and Afghanistan, UAVs have proved invaluable in monitoring enemy activity in real time, and relaying that information to intelligence analysts and commanders on the ground.

And drone aircraft are no longer limited to the surveillance mission. With the addition of Hellfire missiles on Predators and Reapers, the intelligence platforms have become killers as well, allowing near-instantaneous attacks against fleeting targets—without having to wait for strike aircraft and helicopters.

Still, there has been one major drawback in UAV operations. For tactical UAVs, wide-angle surveillance is typically limited to a few square blocks, and that area decreases as sensor operators zoom into specific targets or areas of interest. As a result, intel analysts and ground troops may miss critical activity occurring less than a mile away, with potentially deadly consequences for allied forces. Other platforms (most notably

Global Hawk) offer wider coverage, but those feeds are not always available for small-unit operations.

Gorgon Stare

But the days of "soda straw" UAV coverage are apparently coming to an end. According to the *Washington Post*, the Air Force is set to deploy a new UAV sensor suite to Afghanistan in the coming months. Nicknamed Gorgon Stare, the system consists of multiple cameras mounted on a single drone, allowing it to monitor movement across an entire town.

"Gorgon Stare will be looking at a whole city, so there will be no way for the adversary to know what we're looking at, and we can see everything."

The system, made up of nine video cameras mounted on a remotely piloted aircraft, can transmit live images to soldiers on the ground or to analysts tracking enemy movements. It can send up to 65 different images to different users; by contrast, Air Force drones today shoot video from a single camera over a "soda straw" area the size of a building or two.

With the new tool, analysts will no longer have to guess where to point the camera, said Maj. Gen. James O. Poss, the Air Force's assistant deputy chief of staff for intelligence, surveillance and reconnaissance [ISR]. "Gorgon Stare will be looking at a whole city, so there will be no way for the adversary to know what we're looking at, and we can see everything."

While there's little doubt that Gorgon is a potential game-changer in terms of ISR, there are legitimate questions about the military's ability to sift through reams of video imagery, and deliver the right frames to the war-fighter at the right time. There's also the matter of trying to fuse drone images with human intelligence reporting, providing a more complete picture of the battlefield.

Accomplishing those goals is easier said than done. The public image of UAV warfare is that of a Predator or Reaper orbiting over Iraq, Afghanistan or Somalia, controlled remotely by a two-man crew sitting at their pilot and sensor operator consoles at a base in Nevada. It's an impressive technological feat, but that's only the operational half of the equation.

The much larger job of monitoring and analyzing data gathered by the drones is handled by dozens of intelligence analysts, some in the war zone, but mostly in the rear area, at places like Langley AFB [Air Force Base], Virginia and Beale AFB, California. Some of the spooks [analysts] monitor the feed in real time (providing immediate feedback to troops on the ground), while others wade through hours of archived footage.

In fact, one of the real challenges faced by the Air Force has been "growing" the intel architecture needed to support the UAV mission. Currently, the USAF maintains at least 21 constant drone orbits in the war zone (and that number is expected to grow). Each mission requires the support of scores of airmen on the ground who must process the information.

Increasing Workload

Creating a cadre of intelligence personnel with the required skills has been difficult. First, there's the security clearance issue; it often takes 18 months—or longer—to grant someone a Top Secret/Sensitive Compartmentalized Information (TS/SCI) clearance. The Air Force intelligence school at Goodfellow AFB, Texas, is one of the longest in the service, for both officers and enlisted. Beyond that, it takes months of on-the-job training before someone is qualified to support the UAV mission without over-the-shoulder supervision.

The steady increase in drone missions (and their data haul) has triggered a corresponding increase in the workload for intel specialists. Teams assigned to UAV or U-2 missions at Langley, Beale or other Distributed Common Ground Station

(DCGS) sites often work 12–14 hour shifts, six days a week. The schedule takes its toll on analysts, as does worrying about what they might have missed. On rare occasions, DCGS support teams have watched in horror as a convoy or patrol they're supporting encounters an IED [improvised explosive device], despite hours of preparatory UAV surveillance.

[While] ... Gorgon Stare brings important capabilities to the battlefield, some officers caution that the additional imagery means little without the proper "context," provided through human intelligence.

But on the other hand, analysts also have the satisfaction of detecting roadside bombs or ambush sites before they can be employed against our troops. So hours of staring at "Death TV" isn't a waste of manpower and resources, as Joint Chiefs Joint Chairman, General James Cartwright, suggested at a conference in New Orleans last year [2010]. Indeed, warfighter requests for UAV support have risen almost exponentially in recent years, leading to that big increase in drone orbits—and the Air Force's scramble to support that request.

While almost everyone agrees that Gorgon Stare brings important capabilities to the battlefield, some officers caution that the additional imagery means little without the proper "context," provided through human intelligence or HUMINT. Meshing those information streams has been difficult in the past, reflecting a long-standing disconnect between imagery intelligence and the human collection element.

According to General Poss, the Air Force is now trying to fix that problem by assigning liaison teams to ground combat units. Their presence is aimed at improving the troops' knowledge of what the drones can—and cannot do—while gaining a better understanding of what ground forces need from the UAVs, beyond the target requests that arrive in ISR collection decks.

From a cost perspective, Gorgon Stare is relatively cheap; the system costs $17 million and it was fielded in less than two years. In fact, the affordability may (ultimately) prove a cause for concern.

UAVs for Law Enforcement?

It's no secret that some state and local law enforcement agencies are exploring the use of drones, assuming that flight safety and airspace control issues can be resolved with the FAA [Federal Aviation Administration]. Once those hurdles are overcome, it's not inconceivable that large states, or a consortium of local law enforcement agencies could purchase and operate their own UAVs, with wide-area systems similar to Gorgon Stare. The video feed from those platforms would be downlinked to state and regional fusion centers.

What might happen to the data after that is anyone's guess, but the potential for misuse remains. In its recent "Top Secret America" series, the *Post* detailed the rapid growth of local fusion centers, which are supposed to merge data from various police and security databases, providing better information for local law enforcement. In the Tennessee fusion center, *Post* reporters saw one spot on a map indicating "suspicious activity." It turned out to be the local headquarters of the ACLU [American Civil Liberties Union].

In other states, analysts were more concerned about conservative groups and what they might be up to—never mind that the "reports" were often cryptic, and of little apparent value. Now, imagine your local fusion center with access to round-the-clock wide area surveillance, minus the experience found in military DCGS nodes. That's one reason that domestic UAV employment must be developed deliberately, to avoid a wholesale trampling of our individual liberties.

We clearly need Gorgon Stare in Iraq and Afghanistan— and even along our borders. The question of using it in major cities or on a regional basis (in support of law enforcement) is another matter, one that bears very careful consideration.

Researchers Are Developing Tiny Spy Drones That Mimic Birds and Insects

Associated Press

The Associated Press is a major American news agency, providing articles and photographs that appear in newspapers throughout the world.

You'll never look at hummingbirds the same again.

The Pentagon has poured millions of dollars into the development of tiny drones inspired by biology, each equipped with video and audio equipment that can record sights and sounds.

They could be used to spy, but also to locate people inside earthquake-crumpled buildings and detect hazardous chemical leaks.

The smaller, the better.

Besides the hummingbird, engineers in the growing unmanned aircraft industry are working on drones that look like insects and the helicopter-like maple leaf seed.

Researchers are even exploring ways to implant surveillance and other equipment into an insect as it is undergoing metamorphosis. They want to be able to control the creature.

The devices could end up being used by police officers and firefighters.

Their potential use outside of battle zones, however, is raising questions about privacy and the dangers of the winged creatures buzzing around in the same skies as aircraft.

For now, most of these devices are just inspiring awe.

With a 6.5-inch wing span, the remote-controlled bird weighs less than a AA battery and can fly at speeds of up to 11 mph, propelled only by the flapping of its two wings. A tiny video camera sits in its belly.

[The hummingbird spy plane] can hover and perch on a window ledge while it gathers intelligence, unbeknownst to the enemy.

The bird can climb and descend vertically, fly sideways, forward and backward. It can rotate clockwise and counter-clockwise.

Most of all it can hover and perch on a window ledge while it gathers intelligence, unbeknownst to the enemy.

"We were almost laughing out of being scared because we had signed up to do this," said Matt Keennon, senior project engineer of California's AeroVironment, which built the hummingbird.

The Pentagon asked them to develop a pocket-sized aircraft for surveillance and reconnaissance that mimicked biology. It could be anything, they said, from a dragonfly to a hummingbird.

Five years and $4 million later, the company has developed what it calls the world's first hummingbird spy plane.

"It was very daunting up front and remained that way for quite sometime into the project," he said, after the drone blew by his head and landed on his hand during a media demonstration.

The toughest challenges were building a tiny vehicle that can fly for a prolonged period and be controlled or control itself.

AeroVironment has a history of developing such aircraft. Over the decades, the Monrovia, Calif.-based company has developed everything from a flying mechanical reptile to a hydrogen-powered plane capable of flying in the stratosphere and surveying an area larger than Afghanistan at one glance. It has become a leader in the hand-launched drone industry.

Troops fling a four-pound plane, called the Raven, into the air. They have come to rely on the real-time video it sends back, using it to locate roadside bombs or get a glimpse of what is happening over the next hill or around a corner.

A New Generation of Aircraft

The success of the hummingbird drone, however, "paves the way for a new generation of aircraft with the agility and appearance of small birds," said Todd Hylton of the Pentagon's research arm, Defense Advanced Research Projects Agency [DARPA].

These drones are not just birds. Lockheed Martin has developed a fake maple leaf seed, or so-called whirly bird, loaded with navigation equipment and imaging sensors. The spy plane weighs .07 ounces.

On the far end of the research spectrum, DARPA is also exploring the possibility of implanting live insects during metamorphosis with video cameras or sensors and controlling them by applying electrical stimulation to their wings.

The idea is for the military to be able to send in a swarm of bugs loaded with spy gear.

The military is also eyeing other uses. The drones could be sent in to search buildings in urban combat zones. Police are interested in using them, among other things, to detect a hazardous chemical leak. Firefighters could fling them out over a disaster to get better data, quickly.

It is hard to tell what, if anything, will make it out of the lab, but their emergence presents challenges and not just with physics.

What are the legal implications, especially with interest among police in using tiny drones for surveillance, and their potential to invade people's privacy, asks Peter W. Singer, author of the book, "Wired for War" about robotic warfare.

Singer said these questions will be increasingly discussed as robotics become a greater part of everyday life.

"It's the equivalent to the advent of the printing press, the computer, gun powder," he said. "It's that scale of change."

Progress in the Science of Biometrics Has Led to Policy Problems

Stew Magnuson

Stew Magnuson is a Washington, DC–based author and journalist and the managing editor of National Defense *magazine.*

The technology has arrived.

The science of biometrics, the identification of a person through his or her physical characteristics, made great strides in the aftermath of 9/11.

Retina scans, voice imprints, 10-fingerprint readers have all benefited from digital technology, and are being used today, a panel of government experts said.

How to manage this information, protect the privacy of citizens and share information across federal agencies that have different regulations and reasons for collecting this data is the hard part, they added.

"There is a lot of gray areas and unknown space as we move ahead," Ben Riley, director of the Rapid Reaction Technology Office in the Defense Department, said at a Center for Strategic and International studies panel discussion.

Biometrics is the science. What to do with all the data is referred to as "identity management."

The policies, laws and regulations, however, are lagging.

And it's a technology that makes some members of the public squeamish.

There are laws on the books regulating what kind of data the government can collect from its citizens. But the last major piece of legislation spelling out these rules passed in 1974.

Unclear Laws

In a foreign battle zone where armed forces encounter non-U.S. citizens, a soldier may have great leeway in collecting data such as fingerprints from captured enemies, suspected insurgents or those seeking employment on a forward operating base. The goal in this scenario is simple: classify people as "friends," "enemies" or "neutrals," said Tom Dee, director of defense biometrics at the Defense Department.

"For non-U.S. citizens, it's really fuzzy on what we have to do," said Dee. There is no such thing as a global privacy act. There are only bilateral agreements.

When a person presents himself at a checkpoint in Afghanistan, for example, he could be anyone from a "known or suspected terrorist" to a CIA official with a high level security clearance.

As far as the military is concerned, "the more data you have, the better off you are" in making the decision to let that person pass the checkpoint or not, he added.

If someone is classified as an "enemy," or has potential ties to terrorism, ideally, the Defense Department should be able to pass the name of the suspect on to the Department of Homeland Security [DHS] where immigration officers can call up his biometric information should he attempt to enter the United States.

The challenges of biometrics are now "less and less technical and more and more policy."

The Defense Department has made the Rapid Reaction Technology Office the lead in ensuring all the services are on the same page as far as sharing biometric data within the military community. Since it is a relatively new technology, officials hope they can avoid the pitfalls of the past when "stovepiped" information systems were created that did not allow different users to share critical information in a timely and efficient manner.

But when and how can the Defense Department share what it knows with other agencies?

DHS, for example, has strict privacy laws. The department is under no obligation to extend privacy protection to non-U.S. citizens when it collects data of passengers traveling between nations, but does so anyway in the name of smoothing over relations with allies, said Patricia Cogswell, associate director of DHS' office of policy. DHS and the European Union have tussled in the past over what kind of passenger data can be collected.

The department is on the forefront of the issue because its officers are often the ones the public interacts with the most, she said. Dee agreed that the challenges of biometrics are now "less and less technical and more and more policy."

Sharing Biometric Data

There are many presidential directives demanding that agencies share information seamlessly, said Peter Swire, an Ohio State University law professor and senior fellow at the Center for American Progress. That's easier said than done.

Some liken the solution of linking different biometric databases to a series of "switches." When a policeman encounters a U.S. citizen and wants to run a background check, only a few databases would be "switched on." A non-U.S. citizen here on a tourist visa might allow for more databases to be opened up.

Gerald Epstein, senior fellow for science and security at the Center for Strategic and International Studies, said federal agencies will have a hard time employing the "different conditions, different switches" paradigm.

There are three government communities gathering and using the data: law enforcement, immigration and spy agencies.

They collect this data from U.S. citizens who are afforded rights under the U.S. Constitution, those entering the nation from abroad who fall under DHS' purview and an intelligence gathering community "that doesn't care about the privacy rights of the people it spies on," he said.

In the long run, these three categories are going to be incompatible, he said.

"We will have a system where we will choose our evils and we will live with them. We are not going to have a system that we're all going to think is optimal," Epstein said.

A federal effort to resolve these issues, nevertheless, is underway.

In June [2008], President [George W.] Bush signed National Security Presidential Directive 59, which established a framework for federal and executive departments and agencies to use "mutually compatible methods" to collect, store, use, analyze and share biometric information of individuals "in a lawful and appropriate manner, while respecting their information privacy and other legal rights under United States law."

[The] most important goal . . . is to educate the government and U.S. citizens on the capabilities of biometrics technology and how and when it is appropriate to use.

Duane Blackburn, the chief White House advisor on the biometrics and identity management issue, said the directive was the result of several years of work.

It has five thrusts: the rapid integration of existing technology to meet critical needs; the advancement of future biometrics technology; the further development of privacy regulations; and the elimination of so-called stove-pipes of information that prevents different agencies from sharing critical information.

Education Is Needed

The fifth and most important goal in his mind is to educate the government and U.S. citizens on the capabilities of biometrics technology and how and when it is appropriate to use.

Until 9/11, biometrics was considered "an interesting little niche technology," Blackburn said. The public knew nothing about it other than what they had seen in highly imaginative movies.

Not only is the public misinformed, those in the industry are as well, he said.

Technologists working on new devices have little knowledge of privacy regulations, and the government lawyers and bureaucrats know little about the technology, he said.

"It's like one group is speaking French and the other is speaking Spanish," he added.

Blackburn unintentionally gave an example of the gray areas when he referred to those classified as "national security threats" and those who are "not legally classified as terrorist threats."

When a reporter pressed him on whether he could provide an example of a person "not legally classified as a terrorist threat," he declined to answer.

"That is exactly what the presidential directive tells us to do." Those definitions are under discussion, he said.

Janet Boodro, senior analyst at the Department of Justice's office of the chief information officer, also mentioned a miscellaneous category where a citizen could find his biometric data put in a file.

The Justice Department keeps lists of "known or suspected terrorists," wanted criminals and "other persons of special interest."

When she was asked who these "other persons" could be, she also could not define them.

"When that information is defined, it will be transparent," she said.

An interagency task force comprising the Justice, State, Defense and Homeland Security Departments as well as the Office of Director of National Intelligence will have until June 2009 to complete its work and define categories beyond "known or suspected terrorists."

A Growing Database

Meanwhile, there are about 56 million entries in the FBI Integrated Automated Fingerprint Identification System database, which is located at an underground facility in Clarksburg, W.Va. More than half are not criminals, but presumably law-abiding citizens who have submitted to criminal background checks because a job application requires it. Some in the criminal database are those charged with a crime, but never convicted.

The FBI last year [2007] gave Lockheed Martin a 10-year, $1 billion contract to expand and update the database.

Despite this large number, six of seven U.S. citizens have never been fingerprinted, some panelists pointed out. The government collecting bodily measurements and storing them in an underground facility understandably makes privacy advocates nervous.

Swire said the numbers of stakeholders in this debate is much larger than the government agencies.

"It's 300 million citizens. It's how biometrics are going to be used, or compromised, or used well or badly in a huge range of domestic functions."

"What does that mean for voting in the United States, for immigration in the United States or for how you pay at the bank in the United States?" he asked.

"Data breaches can happen and fingerprints being compromised is a problem," he said.

If collecting fingerprints to verify an identity becomes the norm, what if someone spoofs them or tampers with the data?

When an identity is stolen, it's already a bureaucratic nightmare to obtain a new Social Security number, he noted.

"It's hard to get a new fingerprint," he added.

Rapid Advances in Telecommunications Technology Hinder Intelligence Gathering

Valerie Caproni

Valerie Caproni is a lawyer who serves as general counsel for the US Federal Bureau of Investigations (FBI).

In order to enforce the law and protect our citizens from threats to public safety, it is critically important that we have the ability to intercept electronic communications with court approval. In the ever-changing world of modern communications technologies, however, the FBI and other government agencies are facing a potentially widening gap between our legal *authority* to intercept electronic communications pursuant to court order and our practical *ability* to actually intercept those communications. We confront, with increasing frequency, service providers who do not fully comply with court orders in a timely and efficient manner. Some providers cannot comply with court orders right away but are able to do so after considerable effort and expense by the provider and the government. Other providers are never able to comply with the orders fully.

The problem has multiple layers. As discussed below, some providers are currently obligated by law to have technical solutions in place prior to receiving a court order to intercept electronic communications but do not maintain those solutions in a manner consistent with their legal mandate. Other providers have no such existing mandate and simply develop capabilities upon receipt of a court order. In our experience, some providers actively work with the government to develop

Valerie Caproni, "Testimony," House Judiciary Committee Subcommittee on Crime, Terrorism and Homeland Security, February 17, 2011. www.judiciary.house.gov.

intercept solutions while others do not have the technical expertise or resources to do so. As a result, on a regular basis, the government is unable to obtain communications and related data, even when authorized by a court to do so.

The government is increasingly unable to collect valuable evidence in cases ranging from child exploitation and pornography . . . to terrorism and espionage. . . . This gap poses a growing threat to public safety.

We call this capabilities gap the "Going Dark" problem. As the gap between authority and capability widens, the government is increasingly unable to collect valuable evidence in cases ranging from child exploitation and pornography to organized crime and drug trafficking to terrorism and espionage—evidence that a court has authorized the government to collect. This gap poses a growing threat to public safety.

Two examples illustrate the Going Dark problem.

The Going Dark Problem

Over a two year period ending in late 2009, the Drug Enforcement Administration (DEA) investigated the leader of a major international criminal organization that was smuggling multiton shipments of cocaine between South America, the United States, Canada and Europe, and was trafficking arms to criminal organizations in Africa. A confidential source informed the DEA that the leader of the organization was a former law enforcement officer who went to great lengths to utilize communications services that lacked intercept solutions. Through the hard work of the agents and with the assistance of a confidential human source, DEA managed to dismantle the drug trafficking portion of the organization. Unfortunately, it was unable to prosecute the arms trafficking portion of the organization, which operated beyond the reach of law enforcement's investigative tools. In that case, the communications provider lacked intercept capabilities for the target's electronic communications, and the government's other investigative techniques were ineffective in gathering the necessary evidence. As a result, elements of this organization continue to traffic weapons today.

In another example, in 2009, the FBI investigated a child prostitution case involving a pimp who was trafficking in underage girls and producing child pornography. The target used a social networking site to identify victims and entice them into prostitution. The provider of the social networking site did not have a technical intercept solution. Although the agents had sufficient evidence to seek court authorization to conduct electronic surveillance, they did not do so because the service provider did not have the necessary technological capability to intercept the electronic communications. In this case, the FBI was able to build a case against the target and secure his conviction using other investigative techniques, but our inability to intercept certain electronic communications resulted in a weaker case and a lighter sentence than might otherwise have occurred. It also impeded the agents' ability to identify additional potential victims and co-conspirators.

While these examples illustrate the nature of the Going Dark problem, it is important to emphasize a few relevant points.

- The Going Dark problem is not about the government having inadequate legal authority—the legal authorities we have for intercepting electronic communications are adequate. Rather, the Going Dark problem is about the government's practical difficulties in intercepting the communications and related data that courts have authorized it to collect.

- Going Dark has been used to refer to law enforcement's ability to collect different types of investigative data. As we discuss the Going Dark problem today, we are not focusing on access to stored data. Rather, we are focusing on the interception of electronic communications and related data in real or near-real time. Without the ability to collect these communications in real or near-real time, investigators will remain several steps behind, and leave us unable to act quickly to disrupt threats to public safety or gather key evidence that will allow us to dismantle criminal networks.

- Addressing the Going Dark problem does not require a broadly applicable solution to every impediment that exists to the government's ability to execute a court order for electronic surveillance. There will always be very sophisticated criminals who use communications modalities that are virtually impossible to intercept through traditional means. The government understands that it must develop individually tailored solutions for those sorts of targets. However, individually tailored solutions have to be the exception and not the rule.

- Addressing the Going Dark problem does not require fundamental changes in encryption technology. We understand that there are situations in which encryption will require law enforcement to develop individualized solutions.

- Finally, addressing the Going Dark problem does not require the Internet to be re-designed or re-architected for the benefit of the government. Within the current architecture of the Internet, most of our interception challenges could be solved using existing technologies that can be deployed without re-designing the internet and without exposing the provider's system to outside malicious activity.

Any solution to the Going Dark problem should ensure that when the government has satisfied a court that it has met the legal requirements to obtain an order to intercept the communications of a criminal, terrorist or spy, the government is technologically able to execute that court order in a timely fashion that is isolated to the individual subject to the order. At the same time, efforts to address this problem must do so in a way that strikes a fair balance between the needs of law enforcement and other important interests and values, such as cybersecurity, civil liberties, innovation, and U.S. global competitiveness. . . .

Legal Framework

In the early 1990s, the telecommunications industry was undergoing a major transformation and the government faced an earlier version of this problem. At that time, law enforcement agencies were experiencing a reduced ability to conduct intercepts of mobile voice communications as digital, switch-based telecommunications services grew in popularity. In response, Congress enacted the Communications Assistance for Law Enforcement Act (CALEA) in 1994. CALEA requires "telecommunications carriers" to develop and deploy intercept solutions in their networks to ensure that the government is able to intercept electronic communications when lawfully authorized. Specifically, it requires carriers to be able to isolate and deliver particular communications, to the exclusion of other communications, and to be able to deliver information regarding the origination and termination of the communication (also referred to as "pen register information" or "dialing and signaling information"). CALEA regulates the capabilities that covered entities must have and does not affect the process or the legal standards that the government must meet in order to obtain a court order to collect communications or related data.

While CALEA was intended to keep pace with technological changes, its focus was on telecommunications carriers that provided traditional telephony and mobile telephone services;

not Internet-based communications services. Over the years, through interpretation of the statute by the Federal Communications Commission, the reach of CALEA has been expanded to include facilities-based broadband internet access and Voice over Internet Protocol (VoIP) services that are fully interconnected with the public switched telephone network. Although that expansion of coverage has been extremely helpful, CALEA does not cover popular Internet-based communications modalities such as webmail, social networking sites or peer-to-peer services.

It is no longer the case that the technology involved in communications services is largely standard.

At the time CALEA was enacted, the focus on traditional telecommunications services made sense because Internet-based and wireless communications were in a fairly nascent stage of development and digital telephony represented the greatest challenge to law enforcement. However, as discussed below, due to the revolutionary expansion of communications technology in recent years, the government finds that it is rapidly losing ground in its ability to execute court orders with respect to Internet-based communications that are not covered by CALEA. Also, experience with CALEA has shown that certain aspects of that law sometimes make it difficult for the government to execute orders even for providers that are covered by CALEA.

Challenges of New Technologies

From a time when there were a handful of large companies that serviced the vast majority of telephone users in the country using fairly standard technology (the situation that existed when CALEA was enacted in 1994), the environment in which court-authorized surveillance now occurs is exponentially more complex and difficult. Since 1994, there has been a dramatic increase in the volume of communications, the types of services that are offered, and the number of service providers. It is no longer the case that the technology involved in communications services is largely standard. Now, communications occur through a wide variety of means, including cable, wireline, and wireless broadband, peer-to-peer and VoIP services, and third party applications and providers—all of which have their own technology challenges. Today's providers offer more sophisticated communications services than ever before, and an increasing number of the most popular communications modalities are not covered by CALEA.

Months can elapse between the time the government obtains a court order and surveillance begins.

Methods of accessing communications networks have similarly grown in variety and complexity. Recent innovations in hand-held devices have changed the ways in which consumers access networks and network-based services. One result of this change is a transformation of communications services from a straight-forward relationship between a customer and a single CALEA-covered provider (*e.g.,* customer to telephone company) to a complex environment in which a customer may use several access methods to maintain simultaneous interactions with multiple providers, some of whom may be based overseas or are otherwise outside the scope of CALEA.

As a result, although the government may obtain a court order authorizing the collection of certain communications, it often serves that order on a provider who does not have an obligation under CALEA to be prepared to execute it. Such providers may not have intercept capabilities in place at the time that they receive the order. Even if they begin actively attempting to engineer a solution immediately upon receipt of the order and work diligently with government engineers, months and sometimes years can pass before they are able to develop a solution that complies with the applicable court order. Some providers never manage to comply with the orders fully.

Even providers that are covered by CALEA do not always maintain the required capabilities and can be slow at providing assistance. Indeed, as with non-CALEA providers, for some CALEA-covered entities, months can elapse between the time the government obtains a court order and surveillance begins. In the interim period, potentially critical information is lost even though a court has explicitly authorized the surveillance. . . .

Challenges to Law Enforcement

State and local law enforcement agencies also face a serious intercept capabilities gap. For the most part, our state and local counterparts do not enjoy the resources, facilities, experience, technical expertise, and relationships with industry that federal agencies utilize to effectuate electronic surveillance. With a few exceptions, they are largely unable to conduct electronic surveillance of any internet-based communications services.

The challenge facing our state and local counterparts is exacerbated by the fact that there is currently no systematic way to make existing federally developed electronic intercept solutions widely available across the law enforcement community. Federal, state and local law enforcement agencies have varying degrees of technical expertise regarding electronic surveillance and lack an effective mechanism for sharing information about existing intercept capabilities. This leads to the inefficient use of scarce technical resources and missed opportunities to capitalize on existing solutions. In addition, there are significant communication gaps between law enforcement and the communications industry: law enforcement often lacks information about new communications services offered by providers while providers often lack understanding of the needs of law enforcement. The absence of effective coordination and information sharing impedes the development of timely, cost-effective intercept capabilities that are broadly available to law enforcement across the country. . . .

The government's consideration of its electronic surveillance challenges must account for the complexity and variety of today's emerging communications services and technologies. This complexity and variety creates a range of opportunities and challenges for law enforcement. On the one hand, increased communications affords law enforcement potential access to more information relevant to preventing and solving crime. On the other hand, the pace of technological change means that law enforcement must update or develop new electronic surveillance techniques on a far more frequent basis, as existing tools will become obsolete quicker than ever before.

Data Mining Technology Creates New Privacy Concerns for American Citizens

William C. Banks

William C. Banks is a professor of law at Syracuse University and the director of the Institute for National Security and Counterterrorism.

With the revolution in digital communications, the idea of a geographic border has become an increasingly less viable marker for legal authorities and their limits. Using the Internet, packets of data that constitute messages travel in disparate ways through networks, many of which come through or end up in the United States. Those packets and countless Skype calls and instant messages originate from the United States in growing numbers, and the sender may be in the United States or abroad. Likewise, it may or may not be possible to identify the sender or recipient by the e-mail addresses or phone numbers used to communicate.

Nor do we think of our international communications as being in any way less private than our domestic calls. Congress apparently exempted from FISA [the Foreign Intelligence Surveillance Act] international surveillance conducted abroad because, when FISA was enacted, electronic communications by Americans did not typically cross offshore or international wires. Now, of course, we do communicate internationally and our message packets may travel a long distance, even if we are corresponding by e-mail with a friend in the United States who is in the same city. The location or identity of the communicants is simply not a useful marker in Internet commu-

William C. Banks, "Programmatic Surveillance and FISA: Of Needles in Haystacks," *Texas Law Review*, vol. 88, no. 7, 2010, pp. 1633+. Copyright © 2010 by University of Texas, Austin, School of Law Publications, Inc. All rights reserved. Reproduced by permission.

nications. As former CIA Director General Michael Hayden said, "[t]here are no area codes on the World Wide Web."

Because FISA was written to apply to broadly defined forms of "electronic surveillance" acquired inside the United States, digital technologies brought the interception of previously unregulated communications inside the FISA scheme. In particular, digitization brought e-mail communications within the FISA scheme. Because of the definition of "electronic surveillance," even a foreign-to-foreign e-mail message could not be acquired from electronic storage on a server inside the United States except through FISA procedures. While foreign-to-foreign telephone surveillance was expressly left unregulated by Congress, coverage of e-mail by FISA created an anomalous situation for investigators.

Officials claim that they need to access the telecom switches inside the United States so that they can conduct surveillance of e-mails residing on servers in the United States. The mined data would necessarily include data of U.S. persons.

Even an exemption carved out of FISA for foreign-to-foreign e-mail would be problematic because it is often not possible to verify the location of the parties to a communication. A broader authorization for e-mail surveillance would inevitably include U.S. person senders or recipients and even wholly domestic e-mail. A foreign-to-foreign e-mail exemption would effectively leave in place the requirement of individual FISA applications for overseas targets using e-mail that rely on an ISP in the United States because government could neither ferret out incoming or outgoing U.S. messages in real time nor ignore those messages.

Changing technologies have also turned the traditional sequence of FISA processes on its head. We discovered after 9/11 that investigators could enter transactional data about potential terrorists and come up with a list that included four of the hijackers—a sort of reverse of the typical FISA-supported investigation. Now our intelligence agencies see the potential benefits of data mining—the application of algorithms or other database techniques to reveal hidden characteristics of the data and infer predictive patterns or relationships—as a means of developing the potential suspects that could be targets in the traditional FISA framework. In order to collect the foreign intelligence data, officials claim that they need to access the telecom switches inside the United States so that they can conduct surveillance of e-mails residing on servers in the United States. The mined data would necessarily include data of U.S. persons.

Terrorist Surveillance Program

After 9/11, President George W. Bush ordered an expanded program of electronic surveillance by the National Security Agency (NSA) that simply ignored FISA requirements. In December 2005, the *New York Times* reported that President Bush secretly authorized the NSA to eavesdrop on Americans and others inside the United States to search for evidence of terrorist activity without obtaining orders from the FISC [Foreign Intelligence Surveillance Court]. Although the details of what came to be called the Terrorist Surveillance Program (TSP) have not been made public, NSA apparently monitored the telephone and email communications of thousands of persons inside the United States where one end of the communication was outside the United States and where there were reasonable grounds to believe that a party to the international communication was affiliated with [the terrorist network] al Qaeda or a related organization.

From subsequent accounts and statements by Bush Administration officials it appears that the TSP operated in stages. With the cooperation of the telecommunications companies, the NSA first engaged in wholesale collection of all the traffic entering the United States at switching stations—so-called vacuum cleaner surveillance. Second, those transactional data—addressing information, subject lines, and perhaps some message content—were computer mined for indications of terrorist activity. Third, as patterns or indications of terrorist activity were uncovered, intelligence officials at NSA reviewed the collected data to ferret out potential threats, at the direction of NSA supervisors. Finally, the targets selected as potential threats were referred to the FBI for further investigation, pursuant to FISA, and the human surveillance ended for the others. . . .

For the first time, surveillance intentionally targeting a U.S. citizen reasonably believed to be abroad is subject to FISA procedures. . . . [But] this increased protection for Americans may be illusory.

The FISA Amendments Act

The FISA Amendments Act of 2008 [FAA], enacted in July 2008, conferred the immunity sought by the Administration and the telecommunications industry, and it authorized until December 31, 2012, sweeping and suspicionless programmatic surveillance from inside the United States. . . .

The FAA does not limit the government to surveillance of particular, known persons reasonably believed to be outside the United States, but instead authorizes so-called "basket warrants" for surveillance and eventual data mining. In addition, non-U.S. person targets do not have to be suspected of being an agent of a foreign power nor, for that matter, do they have to be suspected of terrorism or any national security or other criminal offense, so long as the collection of foreign intelligence is a significant purpose of the surveillance. Potential targets could include, for example, a non-governmental organization, a media group, or a geographic region. That the targets may be communicating with innocent persons inside the United States is not a barrier to surveillance.

For the first time, surveillance intentionally targeting a U.S. citizen reasonably believed to be abroad is subject to FISA procedures. As a practical matter, this increased protection for Americans may be illusory. The government may not target a particular U.S. person's international communications pursuant to its programmatic authorizations, whether the person is in the United States or abroad. Yet officials could authorize broad surveillance, for example, of all international communications of the residents of Detroit on the rationale that they were targeting foreign terrorists who may be communicating with persons in a city with a large Muslim population. . . .

Although details of the implementation of the program authorized by the FAA are not known, a best guess is the government uses a broad vacuum-cleaner-like first stage of collection, focusing on transactional data, where wholesale interception occurs following the development and implementation of filtering criteria. Then NSA engages in a more particularized collection of content after analyzing mined data.

Incidental acquisition of the communications of U.S. persons inside the United States inevitably occurs due to the difficulty of ascertaining a target's location and because targets abroad may communicate with innocent U.S. persons. The FAA does nothing to assure U.S. persons whose communications are incidentally acquired that the collected information will not be retained by the government. . . .

The government may compile databases containing foreign intelligence information from or about U.S. persons, retain the information indefinitely, and then search the databases for information about specific U.S. persons. . . .

Long-term congressional authorization for programmatic surveillance marks a stark change in FISA. The FAA permits collection without any showing of individualized suspicion (except for U.S. persons targeted abroad) even where collection of U.S. citizens' communications is the foreseeable consequence of the program orders. It may be that individualized FISA applications and their foreign agency or lone-wolf probable-cause determinations are relics of the pre-digital age. Congress and the Executive Branch should confront the realities of digital surveillance and develop approval procedures, minimization safeguards, and judicial and legislative oversight mechanisms to govern the use of data mining and related surveillance techniques to better ensure that programmatic surveillance protects our security and our liberties. . . .

Location Markers Are Outdated

It is time to replace location of a target as a marker for regulation. Just as our national security interests and threats transcend borders, our personal liberties, including free expression and privacy, are expressed globally. If neither security nor personal freedoms are advanced by adhering to the traditional dividing line that prescribes authorities for warrantless electronic surveillance, it is time to find another approach.

One problem, of course, is that foreigners abroad are consumers of U.S. cyberspace. When corresponding with another foreigner, these persons are unprotected by the Fourth Amendment if they lack other ties with the United States. There is no reason to limit our intelligence agencies in surveillance of those communications, and the FAA facilitates that collection. Yet if we unleash surveillance at U.S. switches, our laws and policies have not yet devised a way to prevent them from gaining access to the everyday communications of Americans, the dominant consumers of those switches. . . .

What Happens to Collected Data?

While simplifying the basic targeting and presurveillance approval requirements will improve the overall FISA scheme, so

much would be left to the discretion of unelected officials that
FISA collection reforms should also focus on postcollection
controls. . . .

Every FAA decision bearing on specific intelligence targets
is made by Executive Branch officials and is not subject to review by the FISC or another judge. Prior identification of targets to a judge protects innocent third parties from being
swept up in the surveillance and enforces the hallmark predi-
cate for government surveillance—individualized suspicion.
The breadth of FAA orders and determinations permits
vacuum-cleaner-like collection from telecom switches, for example. Once collected, executive officials cull through the data
in pursuit of suspicious indicators that merit further investigation. False positives are one inevitable result. Another is the
potential for abuses of stored data. . . .

By its nature, the FAA shifts nearly all the burden of civil
liberties protection to postcollection minimization, and there
is no publicly known mechanism for tailoring minimization
to these new conditions. Executive Branch personnel select
which communications are retained and, thus, logged and indexed in some way for ease of retrieval, all without judicial
supervision. Relying on the default requirements, by following
FAA minimization procedures the government could compile
databases of collected information, maintain them, and search
them later for information about U.S. persons.

Minimization requirements should be reviewed alongside
the predictive abilities of the data-mining methods employed
in programmatic surveillance. In 2008, a committee of the
National Research Council found that "automated identification of terrorists through data mining is neither feasible as an
objective nor desirable as a goal of technology development
efforts." . . .

The National Research Council acknowledged that traditional minimization "has been rendered largely irrelevant in
recent years as technology and applications have evolved so

that vast streams of data are recorded and stored, rather than just limited, relevant elements. . . . Even irrelevant data are routinely retained by the government indefinitely." The Council recommends that "[w]henever practicable" personal identifying information should be "removed, encrypted, or otherwise obscured" before retention or dissemination. . . .

We should worry less about what is collected and how and more about how what is collected is used.

During the pre-enactment hearings on FISA more than thirty years ago, Congress recognized that there are "a number of means and techniques which the minimization procedures may require to achieve the purpose set out in the definition." The FISA practice of retaining foreign intelligence has relied on selective logging and indexing of information. The FISC, in its 2002 *In re All Matters* opinion, closely examined the retention stage, and concluded that the critical determination is when "a reviewing official, usually an FBI case agent, makes an informed judgment as to whether the information seized is or might be foreign intelligence information related to clandestine intelligence activities or international terrorism." If the case agent decides that there is no foreign intelligence information in what is being reviewed, minimization would leave the recorded information off the indexing table: "if recorded, the information would not be indexed, and thus become non-retrievable; if in hard copy, from facsimile intercept or computer print-out, it should be discarded; if on re-recordable media, it could be erased; or if too bulky or too sensitive, it might be destroyed." Over time, criminal appeals where FISA surveillance was alleged to have been conducted unlawfully revealed that minimized information may nonetheless have been recorded and not destroyed and may remain in some electronic format available for retrieval. . . .

The Need for Controls

When I first became a student of FISA, more than twenty years ago, I struggled to understand when a friend who worked inside the FISA process told me that we should worry less about what is collected and how and more about how what is collected is used. Eventually I learned about the importance of the now-lowered wall that separated foreign intelligence from law enforcement and about how minimization could protect private information.

Meanwhile the digital revolution and our data-driven society resulted in private industry having access to personal identifying information about most Americans. The constitutional and statutory law grew up around the premise that our voluntary sharing of that personal information with our credit card companies, ISPs [Internet service providers], and banks eliminated any reasonable expectation of privacy in that information. When the government more prominently and aggressively began collecting and then mining that stream of data, especially after September 11, only a few limits were set on its use. Yet, when the TSP was exposed based on the same techniques, there was widespread condemnation of the Bush Administration. Why?

Part of the reason is that Americans did not know that the government could be listening in on or viewing their international telecommunications traffic, incoming and outgoing, and we feared that our conversations and emails were being monitored by someone at NSA. Once we learned more about the program, we also feared that officials were continuing to monitor our communications without probable cause and without the approval of any judge.

As we learned more about TSP and its follow-on iterations, as authorized by the FISC and then Congress, it became clear that the more significant privacy intrusion occurs not at the initial stage of flagging our calls or e-mails, but at the point when someone, looking at aggregate data for patterns or suspicious activity, decides to personally review an individual's communications. In other words, we should be worried more about what the data is used for, not so much that it is collected.

CHAPTER 4

Should Those Who Leak Government Secrets Be Prosecuted?

Overview: Government Workers Who Leak Secret Information Are Facing Criminal Charges

Josh Gerstein

Josh Gerstein is a White House reporter for the online magazine Politico, *specializing in legal and national security issues.*

The [Barack] Obama administration, which famously pledged to be the most transparent in American history, is pursuing an unexpectedly aggressive legal offensive against federal workers who leak secret information to expose wrongdoing, highlight national security threats or pursue a personal agenda.

In just over two years since President Barack Obama took office, prosecutors have filed criminal charges in five separate cases involving unauthorized distribution of classified national security information to the media. And the government is now mulling what would be the most high-profile case of them all—prosecuting WikiLeaks [a website that publishes secret documents] founder Julian Assange

That's a sharp break from recent history, when the U.S. government brought such cases on three occasions in roughly 40 years.

The government insists it's only pursuing individuals who act with reckless disregard for national security, and that it has an obligation to protect the nation's most sensitive secrets from being revealed. Anyone seeking to expose malfeasance has ample opportunity to do so through proper channels, government lawyers say.

But legal experts and good-government advocates say the hard-line approach to leaks has a chilling effect on whistle-blowers, who fear harsh legal reprisals if they dare to speak up.

Not only that, these advocates say, it runs counter to Obama's pledges of openness by making it a crime to shine a light on the inner workings of government—especially when there are measures that could protect the nation's interests without hauling journalists into court and government officials off to jail.

"It is not to me a good sign when government chooses to go after leakers using the full force of criminal law when there are other ways to handle these situations," said Jane Kirtley, a University of Minnesota law professor and former executive director of the Reporters Committee for Freedom of the Press. "Of course, the government has to have some kind of remedy, [but] I'd certainly hope they're being very selective about these prosecutions."

Jesselyn Radack, a former Justice Department attorney now with the Government Accountability Project, said it's "very destructive and damaging to be going after people for leaks that embarrass the government." The policy, she said, is "a disturbing one particularly from a president who got elected pledging openness and transparency—and someone who also got elected thanks to a lot of [Bush-era] scandals that were revealed by whistleblowers."

But Jack Goldsmith, a senior Justice Department official under President George W. Bush, said the U.S. intelligence apparatus—which is perhaps most at risk from leaks of classified information—has pressured Obama's Justice Department to get tough.

"Leaking has gotten a lot worse over the last decade," said Goldsmith, now a law professor at Harvard. "It's viewed as sort of a crisis in the intelligence community in the sense that there is a strong perceived need to do something about it."

A Double Standard

Yet Goldsmith notes an apparent double standard: top White House and administration officials give unauthorized information to Washington reporters almost daily, but authorities will come down hard if rank-and-file employees get caught doing the same thing. "Top officials frequently leak classified information and nothing happens to them," he said.

> *The campaign here [in America] against whistleblowers is actually unprecedented in legal terms.*

Still, leak prosecutions brought under Obama amount to "almost twice as many as all previous presidents put together," noted Daniel Ellsberg, who changed history and helped set a legal precedent when he handed the Pentagon's top-secret assessment of the Vietnam War to *New York Times* reporters four decades ago. "The campaign here against whistleblowers is actually unprecedented in legal terms."

The stakes in the White House's anti-leak drive could rise higher if the Justice Department decides to prosecute WikiLeaks' Assange for facilitating the publication of hundreds of thousands of classified U.S. military reports from Iraq and Afghanistan, along with thousands of sensitive cables from American diplomats overseas. Prosecuting the enigmatic Australian, however, is easier said than done.

Trying to extradite Assange and haul him into a U.S. court is certain to ignite hot debate over First Amendment protections and raise questions about whether mainstream journalists will be the next targets for prosecution. But if the Obama administration doesn't move against Assange, it could spur outrage in the intelligence community and bipartisan anger on Capitol Hill.

It's hard to say how much of the campaign to punish leakers stems from the current administration's desire to make it a priority and how much stems simply from the glacial-paced investigation of cases left over from Bush's term. Two of the five prosecutions brought since Obama took office pertain to alleged leaks that sprung under his predecessor.

The Bush-era cases include former National Security Agency official Thomas Drake, who is set to stand trial next month [April 2011] in a case stemming from leaks that led to *Baltimore Sun* articles in 2006 and 2007 about alleged waste in classified NSA surveillance programs. In September, former Central Intelligence Agency officer Jeffrey Sterling is scheduled to go on trial for allegedly leaking information about a botched CIA covert operation to sabotage Iran's reputed nuclear weapons program—a plot disclosed in *Times* reporter James Risen's 2006 book, "State of War."

Another three prosecutions relate to leaks on Obama's watch, however, including the case of Army Private Bradley Manning—perhaps the highest-profile leak case in American history. Manning, a boyish, 23-year-old intelligence analyst, allegedly helped Assange and WikiLeaks obtain hundreds of thousands of military reports and diplomatic cables, many of them classified.

The military filed more charges against Manning last week [early March 2011] including a count of aiding the enemy—a capital offense, though prosecutors say they won't seek the death penalty.

Justice Department spokesman Matt Miller declined to comment on whether the Obama administration is taking a tougher line against leakers, but said "we take the leaking of classified information very seriously." However, court documents indicate that punishing leakers seems to have become a higher priority.

More Dangerous than Spying

In a brief filed in January seeking to deny Sterling bail, prosecutors argued that leaking is more pernicious and harmful to national security than old-school, cash-for-info spying. Unlike an intelligence swap or document transaction with a foreign agent, prosecutors wrote, Sterling "elected to disclose the classified information publicly through the mass media" where any U.S. enemy could read it, "thus posing an even greater threat to society."

Nevertheless, despite talk of a scorched-earth campaign against leakers, there have been no charges filed in connection with some of the most significant secrets revealed during the past decade—including disclosures to the *New York Times* about the Bush-era effort to intercept some phone calls and e-mails without warrants.

The lack of charges over the warrantless wiretapping leak, which hit the front page of the *Times* in December 2005, is particularly notable since former Justice Department attorney Thomas Tamm told *Newsweek* more than two years ago that he was a key source for the story.

"He basically put a target on his head and said, 'Come get me,'" said Steven Aftergood, with the Federation of American Scientists' Project on Government Secrecy. "And they didn't."

In addition, there have been no prosecutions or even signs of serious investigation into a large volume of classified leaks to *Washington Post* reporter Bob Woodward for the books he has written on war policy under both recent White Houses. *POLITICO* reported last year that Woodward sometimes arrived for official interviews carrying classified maps.

While the Obama administration has, like its predecessors, steered clear thus far of charging journalists with receiving or publishing classified information, it has not shied away from using the courts to pry out information about a reporter's sources. Last year, the Justice Department re-issued a grand jury subpoena to Risen in an apparent effort to determine his sources for the Iran nuclear story. Attorney General Eric Holder is believed to have personally authorized the subpoena, since under department rules, decisions to subpoena reporters are made at the highest level.

"I was extremely surprised that the Risen subpoena was reinstituted. That struck me as a battle that no one needed to have," Hearst Corp. general counsel Eve Burton, a veteran of First Amendment court fights told *POLITICO* after word of the subpoena emerged last year. "I thought Eric Holder would be a more moderating force in that regard."

A judge later quashed the subpoena at Risen's request, heading off a confrontation that could well have resulted in him going to jail to maintain his silence.

Pressure for Action

The Obama administration's angst over leaks begins at the top. In private White House meetings, the president has reportedly railed against disclosure of national security information, including the breaches that dogged his review of the U.S. Afghanistan/Pakistan policy in 2009. After one eruption from the president, National Counterintelligence Executive Bear Bryant was ordered to come up with new ways to plug the leaks.

Officials have been tight-lipped about Bryant's review, but a source told *POLITICO* the administration will use not only the law but also employee discipline procedures and classified clearance cancellations to punish the suspects.

Century-old statutes for dealing with national security information need to be updated.

Some lawyers also believe that pressure from both parties in Congress, about WikiLeaks in particular, is driving the administration's tough line.

"This is worse than Ames and Hanssen combined because of the totality of the information," said House Intelligence Committee Chairman Mike Rogers (R-Mich.), referring to former CIA analyst Aldrich Ames and former FBI agent Robert Hanssen, both of whom are serving life terms for spying for Russia.

Rogers said century-old statutes for dealing with national security information need to be updated.

Already, Sens. John Ensign (R-Nev), Scott Brown (R-Mass.), Joe Lieberman (I-Conn.) and House Homeland Security Committee Chairman Peter King (R-N.Y.) have proposed a bill that would make it a crime to disclose the name of a classified U.S. source or informant. And Sen. Ben Cardin (D-Md.) has drafted legislation that would make it easier to charge and convict leakers.

An aide to Cardin called his measure "a balanced approach" and said it would enhance whistleblower protections, but critics warned Cardin's bill edges close to Britain's Official Secrets Act—a statute that makes it a crime to leak anything the government designates as secret.

"Sen. Cardin disavows the Official Secrets Act label, but the fact is that his bill would sanctify whatever is classified," Aftergood said. "The bill says that whatever is classified is presumptively properly classified. That does not correspond to anyone's experience of classification policy. Not even the president believes that. . . . So, why write it into law?"

Aftergood said that if the law passed it would discourage what he termed "good leaks," which expose government wrongdoing or abuse.

"The downside is very serious," he said. "Should disclosure of prisoner abuse at Abu Ghraib prison [in Iraq] have been a felony just because the information was classified at the time? Should the disclosure of domestic surveillance that violated the Foreign Intelligence Surveillance Act have been a felony? I say, no. By failing to allow for the possibility of good leaks, the bill sweeps too broadly."

Those Who Disclose National Defense Information Should Be Prosecuted If the Leak Is Damaging

Gabriel Schoenfeld

Gabriel Schoenfeld, a former senior editor of Commentary *magazine, is a senior fellow at the Hudson Institute and the author of several books, as well as many articles in major national media.*

I've returned alive from my debate with Walter Pincus of the *Washington Post*. He is a genial fellow (as am I) and it was a friendly discussion. As I noted here on Tuesday [June 3, 2008], the proposition under discussion was:

> RESOLVED: That in a free society the people need to know what their government is doing, so the media should have discretion in deciding whether or not to publish "leaked" classified national security information.

Pincus made the affirmative case and I was supposed to make the negative one. But I didn't. As I wrote here:

> I also favor the proposition. If that is how the issue is framed, there won't be much debate. Given the huge amount of material the government classifies but which it shouldn't classify, it would be hard to argue otherwise. Here, for example, is a link to a recently declassified photograph of a handgun. Why it was classified in the first place is a mystery. If Walter Pincus has published this picture, back when it was stamped secret, on the front page of his newspaper, I would not have been troubled in the least.

But that said, I also believe—and here is where I imagine I will part company with Pincus—that if the press is to enjoy discretion in this area, prosecutors should also enjoy discretion of their own.

They should remain free to investigate damaging leaks by subpoenaing journalists and compelling them, under pain of contempt citations, to disgorge their confidential sources. On some rarer occasions, when the press itself violates statutes governing the publication of classified information, journalists themselves should be vulnerable to prosecution.

In response to this line of argument, I received a thoughtful comment from Lawrence Kramer who wrote:

I don't believe it is ever right to enact legislation under which an act "may" be criminal. Prosecutorial discretion refers to the prosecutor's husbanding of resources—to declining to prosecute what is clearly illegal where there is no public interest to be served (e.g., the office superbowl pool); it does not refer to a discretion to decide whether an act is a crime. Yes, the prosecutor is charged with determining whether an act is a crime, but it is not something about which he has discretion. The law says whether the act is a crime; the prosecutor then must decide in his discretion whether to prosecute it. You are advocating a law under which the prosecutor decides whether a crime has been committed in the first place. I believe such a situation might fairly be called a "government of men."

I'm not suggesting I have a solution to the excesses of a free press, only that you don't have one either.

The Espionage Act Is Vague

I am not sure that Mr. Kramer and I disagree about anything here, although perhaps he will see a point of discord. Some of the relevant statutes are quite vague, especially the Espionage Act of 1917. This law does not punish the unauthorized disclosure of "classified" information. Rather, it enjoins the unauthorized disclosure of "national defense information" (NDI). This distinction gives the press a great deal of latitude. In any given case, journalists can argue that information it has published is *not* NDI, and has been improperly classified by the government. Such improper classification happens frequently, and it is easy to dig up examples of information that is not NDI and improperly classified "confidential" or "secret."

Not every leak of classified information is damaging. But some of those that are damaging could be prosecuted under existing law.

Thus, inevitably, the press does have discretion to publish when its comes upon classified information. That has certainly become the common practice in American journalism. Given that the classification system is so haphazard, it would be difficult to alter the practice without radically altering the entire scheme under which information is deemed secret by the government.

But since we are faced with a press that is not only eager to publish classified information, but classified information about highly sensitive and operational counterterrorism programs, some remedy is needed. And that is where prosecutorial discretion comes in. Not every leak of classified information is damaging. But some of those that are damaging could be prosecuted under existing law.

Here in New York City, the police typically do not go after jay-walkers. But a jay-walker trying to cross high-speed traffic on the Long Island Expressway, endangering motorists and himself alike, deserves to be arrested and prosecuted to the full extent of the law. And indeed, not only deserves to be arrested, but in all likelihood would be arrested by the NYPD [New York Police Department].

A similar fate should await high-speed publishers of leaked NDI, like James Risen of *New York Times* [known for reporting on activities of the CIA].

WikiLeaks Has Done Great Damage and Must Be Shut Down

Marc A. Thiessen

Marc A. Thiessen is a visiting fellow with the American Enterprise Institute and writes a weekly column for the Washington Post.

Let's be clear: WikiLeaks is not a news organization; it is a criminal enterprise. Its reason for existence is to obtain classified national security information and disseminate it as widely as possible—including to the United States' enemies. These actions are likely a violation of the Espionage Act, and they arguably constitute material support for terrorism. The Web site must be shut down and prevented from releasing more documents—and its leadership brought to justice. WikiLeaks' founder, Julian Assange, proudly claims to have exposed more classified information than all the rest of the world press combined. He recently told the *New Yorker*, he understands that innocent people may be hurt by his disclosures ("collateral damage" he called them) and that WikiLeaks might get "blood on our hands."

With his unprecedented release of more than 76,000 secret documents last week [in early August 2010], he may have achieved this. The [*Washington*] *Post* found that the documents exposed at least one U.S. intelligence operative and identified about 100 Afghan informants—often including the names of their villages and family members. A Taliban spokesman said the group is scouring the WikiLeaks Web site for information to find and "punish" these informers.

Beyond getting people killed, WikiLeaks' actions make it less likely that Afghans and foreign intelligence services (whose reports WikiLeaks also exposed) will cooperate with the United States in the future. And, as former CIA director Mike Hayden has pointed out, the disclosures are a gift to adversary intelligence services, and they will place a chill on intelligence sharing within the United States government. The harm to our national security is immeasurable and irreparable.

WikiLeaks's Founder Should Be Arrested

And WikiLeaks is preparing to do more damage. Assange claims to be in possession of 15,000 even more sensitive documents, which he is reportedly preparing to release. . . . Defense Secretary Robert M. Gates told ABC News that Assange had a "moral culpability" for the harm he has caused. Well, the [Barack] Obama administration has a moral responsibility to stop him from wreaking even more damage.

Assange is a non-U.S. citizen operating outside the territory of the United States. This means the government has a wide range of options for dealing with him. It can employ not only law enforcement but also intelligence and military assets to bring Assange to justice and put his criminal syndicate out of business.

The first step is for the Justice Department to indict Assange. Such an indictment could be sealed to prevent him from knowing that the United States is seeking his arrest. The United States should then work with its international law enforcement partners to apprehend and extradite him.

Assange seems to believe, incorrectly, that he is immune to arrest so long as he stays outside the United States. He leads a nomadic existence, operating in countries such as Sweden, Belgium and Iceland, where he believes he enjoys the protection of "beneficial laws." (He recently worked with the Icelandic parliament to pass legislation effectively making the country a haven for WikiLeaks). The United States should make clear that it will not tolerate any country—and particularly NATO [North Atlantic Treaty Organization] allies such as Belgium and Iceland—providing safe haven for criminals who put the lives of NATO forces at risk.

With appropriate diplomatic pressure, these governments may cooperate in bringing Assange to justice. But if they refuse, the United States can arrest Assange on their territory without their knowledge or approval. In 1989, the Justice Department's Office of Legal Counsel issued a memorandum entitled "Authority of the Federal Bureau of Investigation to Override International Law in Extraterritorial Law Enforcement Activities."

This memorandum declares that "the FBI may use its statutory authority to investigate and arrest individuals for violating United States law, even if the FBI's actions contravene customary international law" and that an "arrest that is inconsistent with international or foreign law does not violate the Fourth Amendment." In other words, we do not need permission to apprehend Assange or his co-conspirators anywhere in the world.

WikiLeaks represents a clear and present danger to the national security of the United States.

Arresting Assange would be a major blow to his organization. But taking him off the streets is not enough; we must also recover the documents he unlawfully possesses and disable the system he has built to illegally disseminate classified information.

This should be done, ideally, through international law enforcement cooperation. But if such cooperation is not forthcoming, the United States can and should act alone. Assange recently boasted that he has created "an uncensorable system for untraceable mass document leaking." I am sure this elicited guffaws at the National Security Agency. The United States has the capability and the authority to monitor his communications and disrupt his operations.

Last year [2009], the Obama administration stood up a new U.S. Cyber Command (USCYBERCOM) to "conduct full-spectrum military cyberspace operations" in defense of U.S. national security. With the stroke of his pen, the president can authorize USCYBERCOM to protect American and allied forces by eliminating WikiLeaks' ability to disseminate classified information that puts their lives at risk.

WikiLeaks represents a clear and present danger to the national security of the United States. If left unmolested, Assange will become even bolder and inspire others to imitate his example. His group is at this moment preparing to release tens of thousands of documents that will put the lives of our troops and our allies at risk. Will President Obama stop WikiLeaks from doing so—or sit back and do nothing?

The Intention of Leakers and Publishers Determines Their Acts' Criminality

Gordon Crovitz

Gordon Crovitz is a media and information industry adviser and executive. He is the former publisher of the Wall Street Journal, *for which he continues to write a column.*

In San Francisco last week [mid-April 2011], some 20 supporters of Bradley Manning spent $100,000 to go to a fundraiser for President [Barack] Obama to sing a song protesting the incarceration of the Army private. The accused leaker of hundreds of thousands of classified documents to WikiLeaks had just been transferred to Fort Leavenworth, Kan., from the more restrictive brig at Quantico, Va. Mr. Obama had to explain to his supporters why there's anything wrong with massive leaks of military reports and diplomatic cables.

Perhaps the Obama administration's dithering about what to do about WikiLeaks helps explain why anyone would defend Pfc. Manning. Julian Assange has faded from the world stage to fight rape and assault charges, and his followers are abandoning him, so this lull is a good time to anticipate his next move.

After the 9/11 failures to connect intelligence dots, the government adopted a policy of sharing information widely. But with some 500,000 Americans cleared for classified documents, more leaks are all but inevitable.

Still, the U.S. can move beyond its current paralysis without criminalizing routine leaks by focusing on Mr. Assange, the self-declared anarchist who created WikiLeaks. His stated goal is to deprive the U.S. government of a smooth flow of information by disclosing its internal communications. "An authoritarian conspiracy that cannot think efficiently," Mr. Assange wrote in an essay in 2006, "cannot act to preserve itself." We'll see.

The Espionage Act requires willfully endangering the U.S. . . . Without focusing on intent, the law would raise serious First Amendment issues.

His former top aide, Daniel Domscheit-Berg, recently wrote a book, *Inside WikiLeaks*, describing Mr. Assange's focus on the U.S. as the "only enemy." Mr. Domscheit-Berg writes that when he tried to make WikiLeaks politically neutral instead of anti-American, Mr. Assange accused him in a text message of "disloyalty, insubordination and destabilization in times of crisis." This striking language comes from the Espionage Act of 1917, which makes it a crime for anyone who has "unauthorized possession to information relating to the national defense" and has reason to believe the information "could be used to the injury of the U.S." to "willfully" release it. There may be very good reason this precise language was on Mr. Assange's mind.

The Espionage Act requires willfully endangering the U.S. It may seem unusual to consider intent in the context of how information flows, but without focusing on intent, the law would raise serious First Amendment issues. Many academics and media commentators—and perhaps overly cautious prosecutors—have missed the point that WikiLeaks is different from the *New York Times*. It's the political motivation of Mr. Assange that qualifies him to be prosecuted. The publisher is not liable for its reporting.

Intent Is the Main Issue

Intent is often the main issue in Espionage Act prosecutions. During World War II, FDR [President Franklin D. Roosevelt] wanted to prosecute the *Chicago Tribune* for its 1942 story about a detailed Japanese plan of attack at sea. It turned out the reporter might not have known the information was based on broken Japanese codes, so there was no guilty knowledge.

Likewise, the intent requirement ended the prosecution of two lobbyists from the American Israel Public Affairs Committee. They'd been charged in 2005 under the Espionage Act for receiving and disclosing information about Iran's nuclear program. The judge told prosecutors they had to show "defendants possessed all the culpable mental states" under the Espionage Act. In 2009, prosecutors dropped the charges, citing the "intent requirements." The defendants wanted to broaden awareness of Iran's threat to harm the U.S.

In contrast, Mr. Assange has a willful mind on all the counts of the Espionage Act: that the classified information could be used to harm the U.S., that the recipients of the information were not authorized to receive it, and that he knew the disclosures were illegal and could harm U.S. national security.

Prosecutors can easily treat Mr. Assange differently from the media outlets for which he was a source. The Espionage Act's requirement of an intention to harm the U.S. provides the clear line. Indeed, no news organization has ever been charged under the law. Bill Keller, top editor of the *New York Times*, earlier this year detailed how his staff carefully filtered the WikiLeaks documents to protect U.S. interests, redacting many names and editing out "any details that might reveal ongoing intelligence-gathering operations, military tactics or locations of material that could be used to fashion terrorist weapons."

Despite months of inaction from the White House, the U.S. is not powerless to deter future leaks. Along with prosecuting Pfc. Manning, the U.S. should indict Mr. Assange under the Espionage Act. This battle to protect the free flow of information within the government against constant leaks is part of an information war the U.S. can't afford to lose.

WikiLeaks Is No More Guilty Under the Espionage Act than Many Newspapers

John Cook

John Cook is a staff writer for the news site Gawker.com.

Attorney General Eric Holder says the criminal investigation into Wikileaks' founder Julian Assange is more than just "saberrattling," and Justice Department officials are claiming he violated the Espionage Act. If that's true, isn't the *New York Times* guilty as well?

The Espionage Act of 1917 is a crazy and spectacularly unconstitutional law that basically makes it a crime to publish anything the federal government doesn't want you to publish: It criminalizes obtaining or communicating "information respecting the national defense with intent or reason to believe that the information is to be used to the injury of the United States."

According to the *Washington Post*, Justice Department officials are contemplating a prosecution of Assange for violating it by taking the cache of State Department cables (not to mention two batches of military documents from the Afghan and Iraq wars) from Pvt. Bradley Manning, an Army intelligence analyst who's already been arrested and faces military prosecution, and publishing them on Wikileaks. The fact that Assange is neither a citizen nor a resident of the United States doesn't seem to bother Holder, who told reporters yesterday that there's no reason to believe that "anybody at this point, because of their citizenship or their residence, is not a target or a subject of an investigation that's ongoing."

If Holder really believes that the Espionage Act is a constitutional law that ought to be enforced—as opposed to a mere pretext for making Assange's life as miserable as possible—then he'd better be prepared to go after the *New York Times,* [France's] *Le Monde,* [Germany's] *Der Spiegel,* and [Spain's] *El Pais,* all of which published the classified cables after being granted early access and were part of a clear conspiracy with Wikileaks to break the Espionage Act.

Assange, under Holder's theory, violated the Espionage Act three ways: He "obtained" "information respecting the national defense" illicitly, which the act makes a crime (we will stipulate here for the purposes of argument that the State Department cables can be said to relate to "national defense" as required under the act, an iffy claim); he "transmitted" that information by passing it along to the newspapers Wikileaks worked with; and he "communicated" it by publishing it on Wikileaks' site.

It's incoherent to argue that Assange and Wikileaks violated the [Espionage] act but that the Times *didn't. Likewise, the* Guardian, Le Monde, El Pais, *and* Der Spiegel *are also clearly guilty.*

The *New York Times* is obviously guilty of two of those three elements of the Espionage Act. It "obtained" the classified cable database—not from Assange, but from [the British newspaper] the *Guardian,* which had itself obtained it from Assange—and "communicated" elements of it both by publishing whole cables and by reporting their contents. (Reporting them, it should be noted, before Wikileaks did—the *Times* had its cablegate coverage up several hours before Wikileaks had its site together.) The *Times* claimed in its introduction to its Wikileaks coverage that it gave the White House an opportunity to request redactions to some of the cables, and that it "agreed to some, but not all" of those suggestions.

Why Are Newspapers Less Guilty?

So if it was a crime when Assange obtained the database, why wasn't it a crime when the *Times* did? The Espionage Act makes no distinctions when it comes to sources of defense information: It's a crime to "obtain [it] from any person, or from any source whatever." Assange got it from Manning, the *Times* got it from the *Guardian*; both transactions are equally criminal under the act. Likewise, if it was a crime when Assange published the cables, why wasn't it a crime when the *Times* did? And how could it *not* be a crime for the *Times* to have published classified data that the White House expressly asked it not to, *hours before Wikileaks published anything at all*? It's incoherent to argue that Assange and Wikileaks violated the act but that the *Times* didn't.

Likewise, the *Guardian*, *Le Monde*, *El Pais*, and *Der Spiegel* are also clearly guilty—if one adopts Holder's view—of violating the act, and they didn't even offer the White House the courtesy, as the *Times* did, of an opportunity to request redactions. Each one of them illegally obtained and published the material, and the *Guardian* illegally transmitted it to the *Times*. The fact that they are all foreign corporations shouldn't stop Holder from going after them, since he's made clear that no one is safe from this investigation "because of their citizenship or their residence." The Espionage Act also has a conspiracy clause, so Wikileaks and all the papers can also have another count added to the indictment, since each was part of an obvious conspiracy to publish the cables.

We asked the Justice Department whether the *Times* and the other papers involved were targets of the investigation, and a spokeswoman responded that "while an investigation is ongoing, we will not comment on potential criminal charges or the direction or scope of that investigation."

We think its fairly obvious that the Department of Justice won't go after the *Times* or any of the other papers involved in the story. But if it doesn't, that's just evidence that its attempt to use the Espionage Act to go after Assange isn't about enforcing laws: It's about retribution, harassment, and rattling sabers.

The Espionage Act Endangers Freedom and Should Be Repealed

Naomi Wolf

Naomi Wolf is a feminist social critic, political activist, and the author of The Beauty Myth *and other books.*

This week, [in early December 2010] Senators Joe Lieberman and Dianne Feinstein engaged in acts of serious aggression against their own constituents, and the American people in general. They both invoked the 1917 Espionage Act and urged its use in going after [WikiLeaks founder] Julian Assange. For good measure, Lieberman extended his invocation of the Espionage Act to include a call to use it to investigate the *New York Times*, which published WikiLeaks' diplomatic cables. Reports yesterday suggest that U.S. Attorney General Eric Holder may seek to invoke the Espionage Act against Assange.

These two Senators, and the rest of the Congressional and White House leadership who are coming forward in support of this appalling development, are cynically counting on Americans' ignorance of their own history—an ignorance that is stoked and manipulated by those who wish to strip rights and freedoms from the American people. They are manipulatively counting on Americans to have no knowledge or memory of the dark history of the Espionage Act—a history that should alert us all at once to the fact that this Act has only ever been used—was designed deliberately to be used—specifically and viciously to silence people like you and me.

Silencing Dissent

The Espionage Act was crafted in 1917—because President Woodrow Wilson wanted a war and, faced with the troublesome First Amendment, wished to criminalize speech critical of his war. In the run-up to World War One, there were many ordinary citizens—educators, journalists, publishers, civil rights leaders, union activists—who were speaking out against US involvement in the war. The Espionage Act was used to round up these citizens by the thousands for the newly minted 'crime' of their exercising their First Amendment Rights. A movie producer who showed British cruelty in a film about the Revolutionary War (since the British were our allies in World War I) got a ten-year sentence under the Espionage act in 1917, and the film was seized; poet E.E. Cummings spent three and a half months in a military detention camp under the Espionage Act for the 'crime' of saying that he did not hate Germans. Esteemed Judge Learned Hand wrote that the wording of the Espionage Act was so vague that it would threaten the American tradition of freedom itself. Many were held in prison for weeks in brutal conditions without due process; some, in Connecticut—Lieberman's home state— were severely beaten while they were held in prison. The arrests and beatings were widely publicized and had a profound effect, terrorizing those who would otherwise speak out.

Presidential candidate Eugene Debs received a ten-year prison sentence in 1918 under the Espionage Act for daring to read the First Amendment in public. The roundup of ordinary citizens—charged with the Espionage Act—who were jailed for daring to criticize the government was so effective in deterring others from speaking up that the Act silenced dissent in this country for a decade. In the wake of this traumatic history, it was left untouched—until those who wish the same outcome began to try to reanimate it again starting five years ago, and once again, now. Seeing the Espionage Act rise up again is, for anyone who knows a thing about it, like seeing the end of a horror movie in which the zombie that has enslaved the village just won't die.

I predicted in 2006 that the forces that wish to strip American citizens of their freedoms, so as to benefit from a profitable and endless state of war—forces that are still powerful in the [Barack] Obama years, and even more powerful now that the Supreme Court decision striking down limits on corporate contributions to our leaders has taken effect—would pressure Congress and the White House to try to breathe new life yet again into the terrifying Espionage Act in order to silence dissent. In 2005, [George W.] Bush tried this when the *New York Times* ran its exposé of Bush's illegal surveillance of banking records—the SWIFT program. This report was based, as is the WikiLeaks publication, on classified information. Then, as now, White House officials tried to invoke the Espionage Act against the *New York Times*. Talking heads on the right used language such as 'espionage' and 'treason' to describe the *Times'* release of the story, and urged that [executive editor] Bill Keller be tried for treason and, if found guilty, executed. It didn't stick the first time; but, as I warned, since this tactic is such a standard part of the tool-kit for closing an open society—'Step Ten' of the 'Ten Steps' to a closed society: 'Rename Dissent 'Espionage' and Criticism of Government, 'Treason'—I knew, based on my study of closing societies, that this tactic would resurface.

A Danger to Everyone

Let me explain clearly why activating—rather than abolishing—the Espionage Act is an act of profound aggression against the American people. We are all Julian Assange. Serious reporters discuss classified information every day—go to any Washington or New York dinner party where real journalists are present, and you will hear discussion of leaked or classified information. That is journalists' *job* in a free society. The White House, too, is continually classifying and declassifying information.

As I noted in *The End of America*, if you prosecute journalists—and Assange, let us remember, is the *New York Times* in the parallel [1970s] case of the Pentagon Papers, not [leaker] Daniel Ellsberg; he is the publisher, not the one who revealed the classified information—then any outlet, any citizen, who discusses or addresses 'classified' information can be arrested on 'national security' grounds. If Assange can be prosecuted under the Espionage Act, then so can the *New York Times*; and the producers of *Parker Spitzer*, who discussed the WikiLeaks material two nights ago; and the people who posted a mirror WikiLeaks site on my Facebook 'fan' page; and Fox News producers, who addressed the leak and summarized the content of the classified information; and every one of you who may have downloaded information about it; and so on. That is why prosecution via the Espionage Act is so dangerous—not for Assange alone, but for every one of us, regardless of our political views.

I call on all American citizens to rise up and insist on repeal of the Espionage Act immediately.

This is far from a feverish projection: if you study the history of closing societies, as I have, you see that every closing society creates a kind of 'third rail' of material, with legislation that proliferates around it. The goal of the legislation is to call those who criticize the government 'spies', 'traitors', enemies of the state' and so on. *Always* the issue of national security is invoked as the reason for this proliferating legislation. The outcome? A hydra that breeds fear. Under similar laws in Germany in the early thirties, it became a form of 'espionage' and 'treason' to criticize the Nazi party, to listen to British radio programs, to joke about the fuhrer, or to read cartoons that mocked the government. Communist Russia in the 30's, East Germany in the 50's, and China today all use parallel legislation to call criticism of the government—or whistleblowing—'espionage' and 'treason', and 'legally' imprison or even execute journalists, editors, and human rights activists accordingly.

I call on all American citizens to rise up and insist on repeal of the Espionage Act immediately. We have little time to waste. The Assange assault is theater of a particularly deadly kind, and America will not recover from the use of the Espionage Act as a cudgel to threaten journalists, editors and news outlets with. I call on major funders of Feinstein's and Lieberman's campaigns to put their donations in escrow accounts and notify the staffers of those Senators that the funds will only be released if they drop their traitorous invocation of the Espionage Act. I call on all Americans to understand once for all: this is not about Julian Assange. This, my fellow citizens, is about you.

The Espionage Act Is Unclear, Outdated, and in Need of Revision

Abbe David Lowell

Abbe David Lowell is one of the nation's leading defense attorneys and has served as counsel to the US House of Representatives.

It makes sense to start with the obvious and important—this nation needs a strong law that makes criminal and treats as seriously as possible anyone who spies on our country; we need to address just as seriously a purposeful disclosure of national defense information ("NDI") with the intent to injure the United States or assist an enemy of our country; and there has to be a prohibition for the mishandling of properly-classified information (which may or may not be NDI).

To address these issues, the differences in these categories—spying (or real espionage), disclosure of national defense information (NDI), and mishandling of classified information—should be set out in separate provisions of the law, each that clearly defines the offense it seeks to address and each with penalties appropriate for the conduct involved. One significant problem with the Act, currently, is that its antiquated structure still lumps or can lump these three separate forms of violation in the same sections of the statute. This neither serves justice well when it seeks to address the most egregious conduct (e.g., a government official who, for money or misplaced loyalty, provides NDI to an adversary) nor promotes fairness when it is applied to lesser offenses (e.g., a government official including classified information in an oral con-

Abbe David Lowell, "Testimony," House Committee on the Judiciary, December 16, 2010. www.judiciary.house.gov. Copyright © 2010 by Abbe David Lowell. All rights reserved. Reproduced by permission..

versation as part of his/her regular work when talking to someone outside of government).

Overclassifying Information

One problem with any law that addresses the improper disclosure of classified information, of course, is the overclassification of information. I realize this is not an issue the Committee is specifically addressing, but it is an important consideration when a law criminalizes disclosure of such material. As one saying goes: "when everything is classified, nothing really is classified." The government's former "classification czar," J. William Leonard, testified to Congress, "[i]t is no secret that the government classifies too much information." During that same hearing, the Department of Defense's Undersecretary for Intelligence, Carol Haave, echoed this point. When asked to assess the rate of overclassification, both Leonard and Haave stated that probably about *half* of all classified information is overclassified. Some agencies even classify newspaper articles and other public domain materials.

Any law would work best if applied to a system that carefully distinguished between that information that should be closely held and that which may be confidential from a policy or political point of view, but not from the perspective of national security. As we can now read in the material released by [the website] WikiLeaks, there is material that is classified presumably because it may be embarrassing to someone (a diplomat's opinion about the private life of a foreign leader) rather than something that is classified because it readily relates to national security (the plan to take military action if a foreign leader provokes a confrontation). Too often, government officials during their day's work find it easier to classify information or classify it at a higher level than necessary because it requires more effort and consideration to do less. No one gets in trouble for classifying something that should be unclassified, but people get in trouble for the opposite. Congress should keep this in mind when legislating a criminal law for the disclosure of what might turn out to have been improperly classified in the first place.

The Current Espionage Act

After WWII [World War II], there was a proposal to enact legislation prohibiting the disclosure of any classified information. Congress rejected this approach, and instead, in 1950, passed one section [798] of the current Espionage Act. Again with reference to the way the world worked 50 years ago, Section 798 criminalizes the disclosure of four very specific types of classified information, primarily relating to the government's cryptographic systems and communication intelligence activities. This section of the law makes it a crime to "knowingly and willfully communicate, furnish, transmit, or otherwise make available to an unauthorized person, or publish, or use," the information "in any manner prejudicial to the safety or interest of the United States or for the benefit of any foreign government to the detriment of the United States."

This section is far from clear. For example, Section 798 defines "classified information" as information that was made confidential "for reasons of national security." So this raises very specifically the issue (and a possible defense) of whether something was improperly classified.

> Digital technology and the Internet have significantly blurred, if not entirely erased, the lines between "communicating," "publishing," and "using" information.

The statute is ambiguous as to whether it requires a prosecutor to prove that each of the enumerated activities—such as communication or publication of the information—must be to the prejudice or detriment of the United States. One plausible reading of the statute, which two courts appear to have adopted, is that where the defendant is charged with communicating or publishing the information, the prosecutor need only prove that the information was classified; by contrast, where the defendant is charged with "using" the information, a prosecutor must prove a risk of harm. This interpretation raises First Amendment concerns, because it lets a jury convict someone for publishing classified information without any evidence of potential harm to national security. And as a practical matter, it makes little sense to apply different standards to "communication," "publication," and "use," because digital technology and the Internet have significantly blurred, if not entirely erased, the lines between "communicating," "publishing," and "using" information.

What is primarily missing in the [Espionage] Act right now is clarity.

Another section of the law that was used to charge the former AIPAC [American Israel Public Affairs Committee] lobbyists [charged in 2005 with conspiring to obtain and pass classified information], prohibits "willfully" disclosing "information relating to the national defense." This Section may be even less clear than Section 798. First, the law does not actually make it illegal to disclose classified information. Instead, it talks about documents and information "relating to the national defense." This is a broad term that could refer not only to things like troop locations and nuclear launch codes, but also to documents whose release would probably benefit the nation, such as proof of corruption in the awarding of armament contracts. Second, 2010 vocabulary is different than that used in 1917—the term today is "national security" not "national defense," and it is unclear how the two concepts may differ. Third, the text of Section 793 treats national defense "documents" differently from national defense "information." As written, the law does not require prosecutors to prove that national defense "documents" pose a risk to the United States, and therefore raises many of the same First Amendment concerns that Section 798 does. And fourth, while the statute does not distinguish between theft and mere receipt of classified information, journalists have and will continue to argue that the First Amendment requires this distinction.

What is primarily missing in the Act right now is clarity. The statute has been attacked often as vague and overbroad (this was done in the AIPAC lobbyists' case). Because of its breadth and language, it can be applied in a manner that infringes on proper First Amendment activity: discussions of foreign policy between government officials and private parties or proper newsgathering to expose government wrongdoing.

To save the law from constitutional attacks, courts have bent and twisted the Act's language to engraft various evidentiary requirements to conform it to both the First Amendment and Due Process Clause. . . .

The WikiLeaks Events

Now the world is focused on WikiLeaks and there is word that a grand jury in Alexandria, Virginia is considering the evidence. If the Espionage Act were used to bring charges against WikiLeaks or its founder, Julian Assange, this too would be unprecedented because it would be applying the law to a (a) non-government official, (b) who had no confidentiality agreement, (c) who did not steal the information, (d) who did not sell or pay for the information involved, (e) who was quite out front and not secretive about what he was doing, (f) who gave the U.S. notice and asked if the government wanted to make redactions to protect any information, *and* (g) in a context that can be argued to be newsgathering and dissemination protected by the First Amendment. If the Act applies to this disclosure, then why does it not apply as well to the articles written by the *New York Times* and other traditional media with the same disclosures? On its face, the Espionage Act does not distinguish between these two disclosures and would apply equally to both and to any even further dissemination of the same information.

The First Amendment Applies

The mere fact that classified information is involved does not mean that the Constitution has no application. The First Amendment is intended to facilitate public discourse and collective decision-making about matters of public concern, particularly government affairs. Words and ideas are still words and ideas even if the Executive Branch deems them too dangerous to be disclosed to the public. As a result, in the AIPAC lobbyists' case, the federal district court judge rejected the prosecutors' categorical argument that when classified information is at issue, the First Amendment affords no protection whatsoever. There has never been a prosecution of a media organization under the Espionage Act, and the issue was a tangent to a few members of the Supreme Court that decided the Pentagon Papers case in 1971 [regarding US policy in Vietnam] (a case brought for a prior civil restraining order, not a criminal prosecution).

The Act's breadth and vagueness can, intentionally or not, result in a powerful chill on the kinds of open government, freedom of the press, and transparency in proper foreign policy formulation that makes this country stronger.

What the First Amendment does is to balance the societal interests in public discourse, on the one hand, and a genuine risk of harm, on the other. When foreign policy information is made public, as was done by WikiLeaks and the traditional press, and as was done by the *New York Times* in the Pentagon Papers case, it almost certainly implicates the type of public discourse that the First Amendment is intended to protect. In addition, the fact that the information was made public could affect the assessment of the damage to national security. In a traditional case of selling secrets to a foreign power, our government may not know for years that classified information has made its way into the enemy's hands, and therefore we take no steps to mitigate the damage of the disclosures. By contrast, when the revelations are as public as the WikiLeaks material has been, our government can at least be certain what exactly it is that our adversaries have learned.

Of course, the First Amendment would not and should not provide blanket immunity, for example, to a newspaper that tips off enemy forces by publishing a story that describes, in advance, a planned assault by the U.S. military on an Al Qaeda or Taliban stronghold. While such a news report might arguably provide some benefit to public understanding of our government, the imminent and likely risk of harm to American troops would far outweigh any such benefit, and that there would be no First Amendment protection for such a publication.

That the same section or sections of the Act can be used to prosecute discussions of pure foreign policy as in the AIPAC lobbyists context, the opinions of diplomats about the private life of world leaders as has occurred in WikiLeaks, and former FBI agent turned Russian spy Robert Hannsen [arrested in 2001 and currently serving a life sentence in federal prison] demonstrates that the statute both sweeps too broadly and also does not properly address the real conduct it seeks to make criminal. The Act's breadth and vagueness can, intentionally or not, result in a powerful chill on the kinds of open government, freedom of the press, and transparency in proper foreign policy formulation that makes this country stronger. It does not serve proper national security or law enforcement interests to have this possibility of improper application of the Act to conduct that was not targeted in 1917 and has even less reason to be targeted today.

Recommendations for a New Law

Accordingly, Congress should revise the Act. It is almost 100 years old and was passed at a time and in an era that has little resemblance to the type of threats the county faces now or for the way information is disseminated today. Even so, the Act was criticized when it was passed and almost every decade later for issues similar to those being discussed now. . . .

As is always the case, a current, big story can be the catalyst for congressional oversight. This is good. A meaningful debate about the Espionage Act and changes to the law are long overdue. However, a current scandal or crisis is *not* the time to act too quickly. There is often an urge to address the clamor of the crisis to show that Washington is listening and doing something and taking a problem seriously. This can lead to ill-conceived laws that have unintended consequences that infringe on rights and cause decades of needless litigation. Indeed, whatever WikiLeaks and Mr. Assange have done, they have done. A new law would not apply to these past acts under the prohibition against *ex post facto* [after the fact] laws. So, the current issues are a very good opportunity to do the careful review and sifting of the national security values we have to protect and balance them against the rights we cherish. There is no doubt that an effective law can be crafted to address espionage, improper disclosure of national defense information, and improper dissemination of classified information, but this will require the kind of painstaking consideration that these hearings have begun, reference to the current case law, the input of the national security community and the scholarly community that will take a little time.

Courts that have grappled with the Espionage Act have been constrained by having to apply its existing structure and language. Obviously, Congress is not so limited. The point is that there is a real opportunity, that these and similar hearings recognize, to create a tough law, a clear law, and a law that also can respect the values we place on a free speech and open government.

Organizations to Contact

The editors have compiled the following list of organizations concerned with the issues debated in this book. The descriptions are derived from materials provided by the organizations. All have publications or information available for interested readers. The list was compiled on the date of publication of the present volume; names, addresses, phone and fax numbers, and e-mail and Internet addresses may change. Be aware that many organizations take several weeks or longer to respond to inquiries, so allow as much time as possible.

American Civil Liberties Union (ACLU)
125 Broad St., 18th Floor, New York, NY   10004
(212) 549-2500
website: www.aclu.org

The ACLU is a nonprofit organization that since 1920 has worked in courts, legislatures, and communities to defend and preserve the individual rights and liberties guaranteed by the Constitution, including the right to privacy. It has over a half-million members and maintains offices in all states. Among its website's many sections are "Protecting Civil Liberties in the Digital Age," "Mapping the FBI: Uncovering Abusive Surveillance," and "Spy Files: Department of Homeland Security."

Central Intelligence Agency (CIA)
Office of Public Affairs, Washington, DC   20505
(703) 482-0623 • fax: (703) 482-1739
website: www.cia.gov

The CIA is an independent US government agency responsible for providing national security intelligence to senior US policy makers. It collects information that reveals the plans, intentions, and capabilities of the nation's adversaries; produces analysis that provides insight, warning and opportunity to the president and other decision makers; and conducts covert action at the direction of the president to preempt threats or achieve US policy objectives. Its website contains information about the agency's history, featured stories about its activities, FAQs, news, speeches, and CIA career opportunities.

Electronic Frontier Foundation (EFF)

454 Shotwell St., San Francisco, CA   94110-1914
(415) 436-9333 • fax: (415) 436-9993
e-mail: information@eff.org
website: www.eff.org

The EFF is a civil liberties group defending the rights of the public in the digital world. Its website contains a complete archive of legal documents related to court cases in which it has been involved. One of the site's sections is focused on surveillance self-defense and includes basic information about the US government's expanded legal authority when it comes to foreign intelligence and terrorism investigations.

Electronic Privacy Information Center (EPIC)

1718 Connecticut Ave. NW, Suite 200, Washington, DC   20009
(202) 483-1140 • fax: (202) 483-1248
e-mail: epic-info@epic.org
website: http://epic.org

EPIC is a public interest research center that works to focus public attention on emerging civil liberties issues and to protect privacy, the First Amendment, and constitutional values. Its website contains extensive information on various privacy issues connected with government surveillance, such as laws, policies, and the use of new technologies; in addition it has an annotated list of links to other organizations and websites concerned with privacy. It publishes a free electronic newsletter, *EPIC Alert*, of which back issues are available online.

Federal Bureau of Investigation (FBI)

935 Pennsylvania Ave. NW, Washington, DC   20535-0001
(202) 324-3000
website: www.fbi.gov

The mission of the FBI, the principal investigative arm of the US Department of Justice, is to help protect citizens, communities, and businesses from the most dangerous threats facing the nation—from international and domestic terrorists to spies on US soil—as well as to investigate violations of federal law. Its website contains detailed information about its intelligence activities and about how the role of the agency has changed since the terrorist attacks of September 11, 2001, as well as about its criminal justice services. Also available are speeches, news, and advice about staying safe from crime and fraud.

Federation of American Scientists (FAS)
1725 DeSales St. NW, Washington, DC   20036
(202) 546-3300 • fax: (202) 675-1010
e-mail: fas@fas.org
website: www.fas.org

FAS is an independent, nonprofit organization dedicated to providing objective, evidence-based analysis and practical policy recommendations on national and international security issues connected to applied science and technology. The FAS Project on Government Secrecy works to promote public access to government information and to illuminate the apparatus of government secrecy. It publishes an e-mail newsletter, *Secrecy News*, of which archives are available at its website.

National Security Agency (NSA) and Central Security Service (CSS)
9800 Savage Rd., Fort Meade, MD   20755
(301) 688-6524 • fax: (301) 688-6198
e-mail: nsapao@nsa.gov
website: www.nsa.gov

The NSA/CSS core missions are to protect US national security systems and to produce foreign signals intelligence (SIGINT) information. It leads the US government in cryptology that encompasses both SIGINT and information assurance products and services and enables computer network operations in order to gain a decisive advantage for the nation and its allies. Its website contains extensive material about cryptology as well as FAQs, news, speeches, and information about its high school work-study program.

Office of the Director of National Intelligence
Washington, DC   20511
(703) 733-8600
website: www.dni.gov

The Office of the Director of National Intelligence serves as the head of the US Intelligence Community (IC), which is a federation of executive branch agencies and organizations that work separately and together to conduct intelligence activities necessary for the conduct of foreign relations and the protection of the national security of the United States. The Director's website offers detailed information about the various IC organizations and the nature of their activity, plus FAQs, news, and links to the kids pages of all the intelligence agencies. The publications *Consumers Guide to the Intelligence Community, An Overview of the Intelligence Community for the 111th Congress,* and others are available to download.

Bibliography

Books

Matthew M. Aid — *The Secret Sentry: The Untold History of the National Security Agency.* New York: Bloomsbury, 2009.

Robert Baer and Dayna Baer — *The Company We Keep: A Husband-and-Wife True-Life Spy Story.* New York: Crown, 2011.

James Bamfield — *The Shadow Factory: The Ultra-secret NSA from 9/11 to the Eavesdropping on America.* New York: Doubleday, 2008.

Joel Brenner — *America the Vulnerable: Inside the New Threat Matrix of Digital Espionage, Crime, and Warfare.* New York: Penguin, 2011.

Simon Chesterman — *One Nation Under Surveillance: A New Social Contract to Defend Freedom Without Sacrificing Liberty.* New York: Oxford University Press, 2011.

Henry A. Crumpton — *The Art of Intelligence: Lessons from a Life in the CIA's Clandestine Service.* New York: Penguin, 2012.

Charles S. Faddis — *Beyond Repair: The Decline and Fall of the CIA.* Guilford, CT: Lyons Press, 2010.

Shane Harris — *The Watchers: The Rise of America's Surveillance State*. New York: Penguin, 2010.

John Earl Haynes, Harvey Klehr, and Alexander Vassiliev — *Spies: The Rise and Fall of the KGB in America*. New Haven, CT: Yale University Press, 2010.

Frederick P. Hitz — *Why Spy? Espionage in an Age of Uncertainty*. New York: St. Martin's Press, 2008.

Richard L. Holm — *The Craft We Chose: My Life in the CIA*. Mountain Lake Park, MD: Mountain Lake Press, 2011.

Ronald Kessler — *The Secrets of the FBI*. New York: Crown, 2011.

John Kiriakou — *The Reluctant Spy: My Secret Life in the CIA's War on Terror*. New York: Bantam, 2010.

Edward Lucas — *Deception, Spies, Lies and How Russia Dupes the West*. New York: Bloomsbury, 2012.

Ronald A. Marks — *Spying in America in the Post-9/11 World*. Santa Barbara, CA: Praeger, 2010.

David L. Perry — *Partly Cloudy: Ethics in War, Espionage, Covert Action and Interrogation*. Lanham, MD: Scarecrow Press, 2009.

Dana Priest and William M. Arkin — *Top Secret America: The Rise of the New American Security State.* New York: Little, Brown, 2011.

Nada Prouty — *Uncompromised: The Rise, Fall, and Redemption of an Arab American Patriot in the CIA.* New York: Macmillan, 2011.

Kevin Michael Shipp — *In from the Cold: CIA Secrecy and Operations, a CIA Officer's True Story.* Tampa, FL: Ascent, 2010.

Daniel J. Solove — *Nothing to Hide: The False Tradeoff Between Privacy and Security.* New Haven, CT: Yale University Press, 2011.

Marc A. Thiessen — *Courting Disaster: How the CIA Kept America Safe and How Barack Obama Is Inviting the Next Attack.* Washington, DC: Regnery, 2010.

Robert Wallace and H. Keith Melton — *Spycraft: The Secret History of the CIA's Spytechs, from Communism to Al-Qaeda.* New York: Dutton, 2008.

Joby Warrick — *The Triple Agent: The al-Qaeda Mole Who Infiltrated the CIA.* New York: Doubleday, 2011.

David Wise — *Tiger Trap: America's Secret Spy War with China.* Boston: Houghton Mifflin, 2011.

Amy B. Zegart — *Eyes on Spies: Congress and the United States Intelligence Community.* Stanford, CA: Hoover Institution Press, 2011.

Periodicals and Internet Resources

Katherine Albrecht — "How RFID Tags Could Be Used to Track Unsuspecting People," *Scientific American*, September 2008.

Pauline Arrillaga — "Chinese Espionage Puts US Secrets in Wrong Hands," CNBC.com, May 7, 2011. www.cnbc.com.

Steven Ashley — "Digital Surveillance: Tools of the Spy Trade," *Scientific American*, September 2008.

Associated Press — "Supreme Court Weighs Legality of GPS Tracking," CBSNews.com, November 8, 2011. www.cbsnews .com.

Gary S. Bekkum — "Thomas Drake NSA Whistleblower Espionage Case Exposes Psychic Spy Connection," *American Chronicle*, May 12, 2011. www.american chronicle.com.

Tom Burghardt — "Orwell 2011: Towards a Pervasive 'Surveillance State' in America Biometrics, Facial Mapping, Computer-Aided ID," Project WorldAwareness.com, March 30, 2011. www.projectworldawareness .com.

Massimo Calabresi — "WikiLeaks' War on Secrecy: Truth's Consequences," *Time*, December 2, 2010.

Whitfield Diffie and Susan Landau — "Internet Eavesdropping: A Brave New World of Wiretapping," *Scientific American*, September 2008.

Sara Freuh — "Preventing Terrorism, Protecting Privacy: The Pros and Cons of Data Mining," *In Focus*, Winter 2009. www.infocusmagazine.org.

George Friedman — "Torture and the U.S. Intelligence Failure," Stratfor.com, April 20, 2009. www.stratfor.com.

Jonah Goldberg — "All Quiet on the Black-Ops Front," *National Review*, October 29, 2010.

Gloria Goodale — "Russian Spies: Hollywood's Version vs. Real-life Espionage," *Christian Science Monitor*, July 9, 2010.

David Greenberg — "The Hidden History of the Espionage Act," *Slate*, December 27, 2010. www.slate.com.

Frank W. Hardy — "Google's Cyber Espionage: A Threat Nearly as Great as Nuclear War," Suite101.com, June 2, 2010. www.suite101.com.

Michael Hayden — "Warrantless Criticism," *New York Times*, July 26, 2009.

Trevor Jenson — "Deception: A Matter of National Security," Operations Security Professionals Association, 2009. www.opsecprofessionals.org.

Ishmael Jones — "'Illegal' Espionage," *American Thinker*, July 9, 2010.

Todd Lewan	"Microchips Everywhere: A Future Vision," *Seattle Times*, January 29, 2008.
Jane Mayer	"The Secret Sharer," *New Yorker*, May 23, 2011.
Nation	"First, They Came for Wikileaks. Then . . . ," December 27, 2010.
Joe Navarro	"Spies Among Us," *Psychology Today* (blog), July 19, 2010. www.psychol ogytoday.com.
Dana Priest and William M. Arkin	"Top Secret America," *Washington Post*, July 19, 2010.
Clay Risen	"Spies Among Us," *American Scholar*, Winter 2009.
Daniel J. Solove	"Why 'Security' Keeps Winning Out over Privacy," *Salon*, May 31, 2011. www.salon.com.
Darlene Storm	"Espionage Act Makes Felons of Us All," *Computerworld* (blog), December 13, 2010. http://blogs .computerworld.com.
US House of Representatives Committee on the Judiciary	Hearing on the Espionage Act, December 16, 2010. http:// judiciary.house.gov.
US House of Representatives Committee on the Judiciary	Hearing on "Going Dark: Lawful Electronic Surveillance in the Face of New Technologies," February 17, 2011. http://judiciary.house.gov.

Stephen I. Vladeck	"The Espionage Act: A Look Back and a Look Forward," US Senate Committee on the Judiciary, May 12, 2010. http://judiciary.senate.gov.
John Yoo	"Why We Endorsed Warrantless Wiretaps," *Wall Street Journal*, July 16, 2009.
Kim Zetter	"Battle Brews over FBI's Warrantless GPS Tracking," *Wired*, May 9, 2011.

Index